CONTENTS

SPOTLIGHT

TRENDS

TIPS

PROFILE

World Inkers Monthly Magazine

Editor: Dustin Pickering

ISBN: 9781946460387

▊ DRAMA

▊ POETRY

Dustin Pickering

WHAT IF THE GODS ARE DAMN FOOLS?

From the Editor's Desk

We must then take initiative. World Inkers Network began with Parrot TV's Literary Corner Youtube program. The show was hosted daily by me, Dustin Pickering, and produced by Mutiu Olawuyi. It coalesced into World Inkers Printing and Publishing at the New Year. This magazine is a fresh start to what we seek to attain in the world of literature for the writers and poets who have expressed support and lent their valuable time. We offer the literary public a one-of-a-kind interview series. In addition, we now offer this fabulous magazine of literary output.

In this edition, we explore what it means to write literature. We also envision the path forward with writings on human rights by Monalisa Parida of India and an article on the prevention of bullying by Abdulloh Abdomominov. Poetic works exploring the magic of love,

ecstasy, the void, and other elusive subjects are included.

Our interview with Ron Whitehead, US Beat Laureate, offers substantial thinking on the meaning of Beat literature. We don't stop there: Carlo Parcelli offers his critique of the Beats in his interview after speaking on them as "social commentators," not literati, on Parrot's *Foreign Policy Review*. Jill Sharon

Kimmelman reminds us that pain is not a hindrance to the creative process after her first poetry release *YOU ARE THE POEM*. Annette Tarpley, admin of The Passion of Poetry, offers some thoughts on being an admin and why she started her own public poetry group on Facebook. Angie Mack tells us about her musical exploration road trip and how she became steeped in blues history. This maiden edition of *World Inkers Magazine* offers a wondrous and copious set of literary imaginations.

As editor-in-chief, I am excited to offer this collection of thoughts, spells, renditions, photos and polemics to the reading public. This isn't an average cheap mag, but a magazine offering insightful literature alongside fantastic contemporary commentary!

***

Available from the publisher

finishinglinepress.com

$19.99

R. W. Haynes
Heidegger Looks at the Moon

These are wonderful poems. In the best poetic tradition, they come alive and prod memories through elegant allusions to classical mythology, literature, and popular culture. Thinkers like Heidegger, of course, pop singers like Sam the Sham, writers like Harry Crews, common folk like Big Jake, as well as literary, classical, biblical and historical characters, populate the world found here. R.W. Haynes' masterful command of language and poetic forms inspires the reader to come on board and enjoy the ride, and we are the richer for traveling along with the poet to Waco or Ft. Stockton, crossing the Rio Grande with Charon, and visiting imagined pasts or literary spaces with Oswald Alving or Chaucer.

Norma Elia Cantú,

Norine R. and T. Frank Murchison Professor of the Humanities, Trinity University, author of *Canícula* and numerous other works of prose and poetry.

DIFFERENTLY - ABOUT SPIRITUALITY AND POETRY

Rozalia Aleksandrova

The Poet lives in the moment of creation. It's more than a smile and a hug. He opens the heavenly gates of Truth. And he enters in Paradise of the highest vibrations to pluck the fruit. And to feed the people.

I have the seemingly difficult task of trying to explain the connection between Spirituality and Poetry in a new plane - that of the new discoveries of quantum and torsional* (information) physics.

About Spirituality.

Many people use the word "spirituality" to express that inexplicable touch on human emotion that challenges them to be better and more understanding of themselves and people. Therefore, in dictionaries, this word exists as an abstract concept - "quality of the spiritual, the presence of spiritual life, spiritual activity." We do not stop there because it is not clear what exactly the concept itself covers, except that it is about life and activity. Let's check what "spiritual" means - which refers to the human spirit, to the mental and emotional activity of man. Here we are much closer to the essence of the concept in its most modern interpretation. Which refers to the human spirit. Although again it is an "abstract" concept. Or not. More than 110 years ago, French scientist Louis Cartan discovered that physics had not yet described and studied the field created by "angular torque" (fr. - torsion). A scientific "trifle" that much later revealed to the world the existence of a fine physical field, which contains the plans for EVERYTHING that was, is and is possible to be. The field of the Spirit. This changes the physical picture of Genesis according to physics from four "floors" to six. And now the picture of the world has changed dramatically. In addition to the known 4 levels: solid, liquid, gaseous and plasma, scientists are also studying the properties of vacuum and primary vacuum. Physics calls them respectively: primary information field and vacuum. And according to church dogma, the 6th level - the primary information field, is called the Holy Spirit. You've probably heard of the "superstring" theory. It studies the constant interactions between these six levels of reality. And he is trying, so far without much success, to penetrate the seventh level - the Creator of Everything. But what is the connection with spirituality and poetry?

Man contains all levels of reality. Including the 7th. The Divine. His visible physical body and the rest of his invisible bodies interact constantly and are "informed" of every thought, word, or action that a person takes. I.e. man is a walking information field, which is a compact sum of all levels of reality. What scientists have found is that all people - humanity - are interconnected through their invisible bodies in a common information field. This was also said by Carl Jung.

Let us return to the definition of "spiritual": which refers to the human spirit. This means that the spiritual, the immeasurable before, is in fact the connection and interaction of each person and all humanity with the Holy Spirit. Man expresses himself through his life and activity. Yes it is. But everything that is not seen and "heard" by society - its intentions, its motives and its life goals - also define it as a spiritual being. I.e. our overall pursuit of the Spirit is the determinant of our true spirituality.

The discoveries of scientists do not diminish the sacred understanding of human values, of his earthly morality. Quite the opposite - Science rises and joins these values, studying them in the name of humanity and divine providence.

What is our connection with the field of the Spirit? With the Holy of Holies?

Through the human soul. Yes, she does exist. It is already proven. As an indestructible unit of every human spirit. Until Atlantis, people have a direct connection to the 6th level of reality. After it sank, they lost it. To understand how human interaction with the primary information field takes place, we need to be aware of what it is and what are the basic laws that scientists have studied for this field. It consists of pairs of inseparable information spirals* in unimaginably low negative values, which transfer information and not energy. They have no mass. Information about each action or observed object is transmitted instantaneously throughout the Universe. As long as she has "ears" to hear her. One can process very little of this information. Around 5 %. There are no barriers to information. None. Besides the lack of senses to perceive or process it. *Today, a person can perceive information to a higher degree only if his own information channels are clean. This means purity of thoughts, actions, words. In everything. Developed, ie. man's pure information channels are today known by the public name of the "sixth sense."*

It is very important to know publicly that in the 4th-6th level of reality the Law of Attraction, of resonance, works unfailingly. The positive is attracted by the positive and the negative by the negative. In other words, with the wisdom of the Bulgarian people - whatever called, the same replied. It has been studied that Man was originally created as a positive information object. In his true nature he is part of the Holy Spirit. The human soul is a witness to this. Of course, and the numerous experiments (hundreds of thousands) conducted by scientists around the world.

Man interacts with other people and with the whole world both through his senses and through the models that society has adopted at a given time in Evolution. Evolution is a basic law of Being. These ideas and statements have been practically proven and studied by many famous and unknown scientists, physicists, mathematicians, psychologists, chemists and others. and more recently linguists. Mathematical research in this area alone is over 40,000 before the beginning of the 21st century.

We can now try to determine the Spirituality of Man.

Spirituality is a real collective information field, an invisible monolithic matrix **, in which the interactions between Man and Spirit take place in every art and every human striving for purity, goodness, integrity, compassion, beauty and harmony, caused by man and supported by the Spirit.

Poetry is one of the powerful tools of Spirituality.

Poetry is, like every object in the Universe, an information field, a unit, a matrix that encompasses every image written or received, a thought that comes to one or more poets as a fine physical field. It contains Universal Wisdom and Harmony. This is real "food" for our subtle bodies. The same that science is called to supply with other human tools. Human logic and human word. Ie Poetry can also be called the Science of the Soul, which has an instantaneous effect on the subtle bodies of man and, possibly, on his logic.

POETRY IS NOT A REFLECTION OF REALITY, BUT CORRECTOR. Through the words that come from the 6th level of reality. It is a science not only for the human soul, but also for all information objects on Earth. Landed, remains in the aura *** of the Earth. *Of course, some ideas that are vital to humanity can be repeated in different versions by poets living in different geographical locations and at different times. This is because some of the poets actually connect not with the higher realms of reality, but with the invisible bodies of the Earth, and draw ideas and images already "taken down from above". This does not belittle today the verses that contain the idea of Love and the unity of humanity as the main engine of our time. On the contrary - life-saving words, feelings, ideas and images for all mankind are affirmed!*

How comes poetry?

Poetry is a Word clothed in words, emotions and INFORMATION from the 6th level of reality. **The mechanism of speech is connected with all the laws of reality, starting with the basic law - Evolution.** But I would rather dwell, because of the need today, on the Law of Resonance. Whatever called, the same replied. You rejoice - you shout Joy. You cry — you called crying. You say bright words - you call Joy, Harmony, Beauty. You use words with negative information - you call them, dressed in the props of visible reality. Not only for yourself, Poet, but for all of Humanity, starting with your family, your loved ones, your people. You remember that we are together. Whatever is happening affects everyone. *That is why in Plovdiv we organize a poetry festival, which has accepted Joy as Poetic credo.*

Poetry expresses itself through the human word **** And it acts through the language of a people, nation, group of people. No language selected. Every human language is important and created from above. Unique. The Divine String of Understanding and Sharing Life is embedded in it. Language is alive as long as those who use it follow the path of Evolution. Poetry is called to preserve life in every language given to the people. And poets help their people honor God and themselves. With the words that pull life forward. To go his own way, predestined and illuminated.

POETIC WORDS CAN WORK MIRACLES IF WORDS ARE ABOUT MIRACLES.

Words are living beings sent to help a person cope with communication not only with others but also with himself. These are subtle energies that shape our invisible bodies in their own image and likeness. And if we take good words as an example, they shape us with a good and bright dense aura. She protects and defends us. The conclusion, I think, is self-evident - Poetry, as a powerful instrument of human and divine spirituality, is the magic carpet of Aladdin, which points us and suggests that the miracles we seek in dream and waking are in us.

* right-spinning and left-spinning pairs, respectively - positive and negative, the whole Universe consists of such spirals and is the densest matter known to scientists.
** matrix is a basic physical concept of an indestructible energy-information field
*** aura - energy-information field of Earth
**** the human word differs from the divine word, but it also has great creative power

Cloud Reflection photograph by Carl Scharwath

POETRY, A THERAPY
Eva Petropoulou Lianou

Poetry is therapy.
Poetry, talks to humans hearts.. Like Angels talk to Jesus..
Poetry belongs to everyone
And everyone belongs to poetry..

Verses are sad
Verses are happy
But feelings cannot hurt
Words are hurting if humans talk bad

Poetry is my language
Poetry unites people
Poetry opens doors
During hard moments
Truth was intoxicated
And nothing make sense

Poetry opened a window
To my lonely life
I find brother and sister
In the other site of the planet

My prayers,
My blessings
We keep the Light

We embrace humanity
Encourage the justice

I am the mirror of your soul
U are the mirror of my soul
We stay united

Poetry is a therapy

WE ALL MUST BE CRAZY

Interview with Carlo Parcelli, poet and publisher

As a Beat laureate, how do you see your poetry evolving the poetry of the nation? How does your lifestyle as poet convey that image?

I never understood the tacit love/hate relationship the Beats had with America. I'm not interested in cultural transgression as they were. I'm interested in intellectual transgression. I've never understood the Beats love affair with Walt Whitman except on cultural grounds. By that I mean he was gay and freedom of sexual expression is a central theme of the Beats. However, Whitman betrayed his sexuality. Granted this was out of necessity. In the 19th century, sexuality between same sex couples was in many ways utterly different from the way we think of it today, still it was largely frowned upon and could carry heavy penalties both cultural and legal. So in ballyhooing American society, its industriousness and vigor, he was praising the very culture that would deny him his sexuality. Further the America he reported didn't exist. Whitman himself did not believe the 'freed' slaves should be granted the franchise. He saw the Native Americans as weak and inferior, a race that would simply dying out. His heyday after the Civil War was called the Gilded Age and run by people we now refer to as the Robber Barons and it was with these Brahmins he dined while they murdered using the Pinkertons and other thugs 30,000 'Americans' attempting to form unions. From 1870 through 1890, Whitman lived through several Wall Street bank crashes leaving tens of thousands people repeatedly homeless and destitute. Any wealth that existed was on the backs of slave and corvee labor. Africans, the Chinese, the Irish, Jews, Italians, immigrants in general and foreign imperial ventures and outright theft of other countries land and resources. In short, Whitman was a fraud and his poetry is a delusion that poets hold onto today to support their own personal delusions about America and its culture. For example, Whitman was a pedophile as evidenced by newspaper reports from his Long Island days as a school teacher. It was even reported at one point he was tarred and feathered. Likewise Allen Ginsberg was a member of NAMBLA. My sense is that American poetry still suffers from the tremendous fraud perpetrated by Whitman which has only been enhanced by his 'cultural transgression'. I'll save a critique of the precious, sheltered, solipsistic tone that flows from Emily Dickinson into much of today's milktoast poetic efforts for another time. In my forthcoming book from Venetian Spider Press, 'Tarrare and Other Poems', I have a 400 line monologue called 'Peter Doyle's Suicide Letter To Walt Whitman' in which my position is laid out in colorful detail.

What do you anticipate from other poets specifically? How do you feel about the business of publishing, selling books, and engaging an audience for self-promotion?

When I was working for 30 years on my synthesis of poetry, western philosophy and science in particular quantum theory using Ezra Pound's Canto technique, I didn't care much about publishing because I was so absorbed in the subject matter itself. Also, my time was taken up with the enormous amount of reading my poetic ambition required. Now, that I work in a dramatic monologue style derived from the English/Welsh poet David Jones, I would like more opportunities to read because, after all, the works are performative while being too intellectually discursive for professional actors to execute.

Everyone today feels they can be a poet. It's just a matter of personal expression. This is unfortunate. More so now that small presses have morphed into self-publishing through huge conglomerates like Amazon. The more poetry published the fewer readers for each poet. Why interest yourself in something you can do just as easily as the next guy? If you write poetry about mowing your lawn, buying Wonder bread or burying your cat, you'd better be prepared to couch such experiences in the most outlandish tropes like Billy Collins or Ted Kooser, or otherwise you'll

"The Beats are not poets; they're just social commentators," Parcelli told *Foreign Policy Review* (January 27, 2022)

do little more than encourage your neighbor who has never read a poem in his life to pen his own drivel and send it along to Amazon. I suppose there are worse things. And perhaps poetry deserves such an ignominious death.

Not that the 20th century's major publishers have a better track record. Poetry for them has at best become a minor tax write off. Small publishers don't have a much better history, but having been poetry editor of my own poetry magazine, FlashPoint, I can sympathize when you feel the pressure to publish something – anything.

I want to engage an audience because I find I enjoy performing. As for selling my work, I prefer to give it away. If you come to a performance of mine and express any interest, even interest in the food scraps in my beard or how poorly I dress, I will most likely insist on giving you a copy of my text.

Your poetics are deeply evolved from the legacy of Pound and the *Cantos* tradition. What does such a tradition enable you to convey that other poetics cannot? When did you decide to approach poetry with the ambitions you sought?

Pound defined an epic as "a poem containing history". This great ambition allows you to know things and synthesize your own theses. But you have to work at it. And be prepared to get nothing in return.

Ironically, the other night a popular sit com was on TV late at night. This particular show jogs my memory about various aspects of physics I once feverishly pursued. The show had a joke about Abu Hamid al-Ghazali's critique of Aristotle which reminded me of how central his thought had been to my thinking in a 45 year old unpublished poem of mine called 'Ontology of Accident.' In that poem I drew on my understanding of the omniscient nature of infinite variables and the nature of accident in al-Ghazali's expression of the omniscient causal imposition of god. My poem also, in part, like al-Ghazali's is a refutation of Aristotle as well as being a meditation on quantum paradox. I had completely forgotten this although 'Ontology of Accident' formed my thesis paper for my master's degree and the great Joyce scholar and co-translator of Greek drama with Ezra Pound, Rudd Fleming, and renowned Pound scholar, Hugh Kenner, were on my thesis committee. So in that sense, I associate poetic ambition with a long, long, long intellectual voyage. Excuse me if I get emotional about the intellect. My work now is a lively evocation through the use of the dramatic monologue riffing off of some of what I've learned and love. As Pound wrote in Canto LXXXI:

"What thou lovest well remains,

the rest is dross

What thou lov'st well shall not be reft from thee

What thou lov'st well is thy true heritage"

EZRA POUND

How do you think younger poets can reach their audience? What advice do you have for poets striving to develop a unique voice?

Reaching an audience? Be as dull witted as they are. If you can do second rate stand-up comedy like Kooser or Collins you're 5% of the way there to nowhere. Tugging heartstrings like a Hallmark card with a few too many words is a sound strategy especially if the experience in the poem never occurred. Be edgy if you must, but make sure the edge is dull like a butter knife.

Submit poems if you must. But understand that the person on the other end probably knows less about poetry than you do. I hear drivel merchants like Button Poetry employ millions of bots to make it appear you've got a plethora of hits.

Unique Voice? I have a unique voice. I wouldn't recommend it to my worst enemy. It's the last thing you want if you want to reach an audience.

The most interesting facet of your mind and personality in my opinion is your ability to critique. By that I mean you have a way of noting and clarifying underlying patterns and assumptions within a work, and highlighting their faults or egocentricities. Why do you believe such a practice is necessary and pertinent?

I think it's necessary and pertinent to point out errors, contradictions, sloppiness and downright stupidity especially if you've been a vocational practitioner for 60 years of an ART like poetry and you actually know a little bit about the topic at hand. Teddy Roosevelt said "Speak softly, but carry a big stick." I speak loudly and bring a big shovel. I'm saving up for a back-hoe and bull dozer in case somebody with talent needs to get through. This is my way of saying that there's a lot of shit and shitters in the way.

A final footnote: To me poetry is sacrosanct. It is the most difficult of all of the Arts to master because at its core is the most complex and unique faculty humans possess. And that is language. If a person who has dedicated his entire life to poetry, criticizes or dismisses your work, it's done for the sake of the Art, not as a referendum on your work in particular. It's just the way we are. It's the way steeped every day in the excitation of the word, in the heightening of the logos, we have become.

***

The Day Thay Died

(For Thich Nhat Hahn)

Kevin R. Pennington

Oh, dear Thay,
I read the news
that you passed away
from this world:
soon, reincarnated
as a Bodhisattva,
guardian of the
Dhamma, herald
of peace, creature
of ultimate compassion.

Perhaps you will return
to Earth again
to continue your work
of spreading non-violence.

I watched you give
Dhamma Talks
on the internet
until you had your
stroke and lost the
power to speak.

You gave the best
advice for someone
with mental illness:
"I think we need more
mindfulness." That
guided with me throughout
the years as I tried
to live by your example.

But as you said in
your own poetry:
no one is ever really
gone, you will linger
in memory and
Dhamma forever.

Kevin R. Pennington is author of Spacetime Nirvana
available from Alien Buddha Press.

Photo of Kevin R. Pennington

RON WHITEHEAD INTERROGATES THE BEATS WITH WORLD INKERS EDITOR DUSTIN PICKERING

World INKERS: Beat literature is about individualism, challenging the status quo, resisting convention. In what way can religion inspire such a lifestyle? In what ways are religious movements themselves expressions of those values? Can embedded traditions also find expression in beat literature?

World INKERS: Tell us something about your own resistance to conventional lifestyles. In what ways did the early Beats betray their ideals? Why should others stay loyal?

World INKERS: Literature can be a refuge of personal honesty, confession, and resistance to oppressors. How does Beat literature exemplify those values in an individual way? Is there anything peculiar to Beat confessional writing that allows it to stand out from historical narratives in literature?

World INKERS: How did the Beatniks change relationships in the United States? How was society developed toward freer ideals by Beat expression, and how can we continue that legacy? In this age of "social change and justice" does Beat literature still have a place in your opinion? How are you inspired by social protest movements?

World INKERS: As you grow older and reflect on your body of literary output, do you find that you see a particular trajectory in that output? In reading your entire body of work, can a reader sense changes in your thinking by periods?

World INKERS: What does the future of Beat mean to you?

Photo of Ron Whitehead by
Debbie Tosun Kilday

Ron Whitehead: Hello! I am honored to participate in the premiere issue of World INKERS. Thank you for the invite. After giving your excellent questions a great deal of thought, and in order to respond both directly and creatively, I've decided to answer all your questions by sharing a piece I wrote with my friend renowned Beat scholar John Tytell. You'll find the answers to all your questions here:

American Poetry and The Beat Generation

UNSCREW THE LOCKS FROM THE DOORS MANIFESTO

The Antinomian Fire This Time

the bone man dances circles

round the subterranean gloom

paints pink and blue and purple

until he fills the room

with the smell of roses

and a pandemonium moon

ANNE HUTCHINSON

WILLIAM BLAKE

There is a struggle going on for our minds, the minds of The World People. Every form of expression is being attacked. The attack is overt and subtle, explicit and implicit. The attack manifests as mind manipulation, as censorship, as fear. The attack is pervasive. Most people, being asleep, are not even aware of the attack - until their doors are broken down. In the face of fear the poet the writer the artist the composer the musician the photographer the filmmaker can and must speak must act. I believe in individuals who are awake who fight for freedom. I believe in non-violent fighting which creates new forms new voices which, by their own being and expression and action, stand against violence against war.

UNSCREW THE LOCKS FROM THE DOORS

UNSCREW THE DOORS FROM THEIR JAMBS

Anne Hutchinson, William Blake, Walt Whitman &

The Antinomian Tradition

VOICES WITHOUT RESTRAINT

"Government shall make no law respecting an establishment of

religion, or prohibitiing the free exercise thereof; or abridging the

freedom of speech, or of the press; or the right of the people peaceably to assemble, and to petition the government for a redress of grievances." -The Bill of Rights, 1st Amendment

Anne Hutchinson, cousin of John Dryden, organized a circle of women and led them in discussions of church sermons. The notion that women would even dare to discuss these sermons was considered subversive - after all, discussion leads to questions. Anne Hutchinson was convicted of "traducing" the ministry and banished, cast out of Boston.

Antinomian emerges from the Protestant Reformation which encourages its adherents to deny authority and resist the state when its moral position is feeble, contradictory, absurd. In legal terminology an antinomy signifies a contradiction which in Walt Whitman's historical moment was the condition of slavery in a supposedly free society. "The attitude of great poets is to cheer up slaves and horrify despots," Whitman wrote. He, like William Blake before him, saw his purpose as spreading to the people the original ideas of the American republic, and a revolution that had been fought to relocate sovereignty in the individual rather than in the state. In an editorial he declared that the greatest evil was "strife for gain," yet even in his crusading journalism he was a voice of affirmation and love.

"Unscrew the locks from the doors,

Unscrew the doors from their jambs"

-Walt Whitman

"Poetry fettered fetters the human race"

-William Blake

"It is not metres, but a metre-making argument that makes a poem"

-Ralph Waldo Emerson

"Urge and urge and urge. Always the procreant urge

of the world"

-Walt Whitman

"through the windr of a wondr in a wildr is a weltr

as a wirble of a warbl is a world"

-James Joyce

When Whitman completed LEAVES OF GRASS, the grass being the uncut hair of the dead, he designed it, set some of his own type, and set as his publication date the fourth of July, 1855.

LEAVES OF GRASS was disdained by critics as "a mass of stupid filth," an example of "New York Rowdyism," "grotesque and uncouth." The only favorable reviews were written by Whitman himself, pseudonymously, except that is for a letter from Emerson proclaiming Whitman's book as the "most extraordinary piece of wit and wisdom that America has yet contributed." After Whitman was debilitated by stroke the young Henry James attacked his work and a generation later, in a jealous attempt to dethrone the cosmic poet who had written the American epic poem of the 19th Century, Ezra Pound continued the attack on Whitman's romanticism.

Whitman revised and expanded his poems for the rest of his life but not before paying over six hundred visits to hospital wards during the American Civil War. Basic surgery was amputation. Suffering was overwhelming. Whitman maintained cheerful optimism, the hallmark of his character. Whitman gave succor to the wounded.

Pound's CANTOS reflect his own lifetime of antinomian resistance to the warfare state. Long after he made his peace with Whitman, Pound became pariah of modern poetry, hysterically protesting "a system which created one war after another in series in system." Ezra Pound was incarcerated, twelve years in the house of bedlam, St. Elizabeth's, an asylum for the criminally insane in Washington D.C., which, years earlier, during the Civil War, had been one of the hospitals for the wounded visited by Whitman.

Another antinomian, arriving in Paris, 1930, with ten dollars and a copy of LEAVES OF GRASS, forty years old, twenty unsuccessful years trying to write fiction during an anguished marriage, liberated himself from the middle class values most take for granted, destitute, surviving by persuading a dozen new friends to feed and house him in rotation in exchange for his conversation, fell in love with Anais Nin, another unknown writer, and began his first masterpiece, TROPIC OF CANCER.

In his poems Whitman simultaneously praised and condemned his country. In CANCER Henry Miller savages America as a "cesspool of the spirit," "a curse on the world." While Whitman introduced orgasmic potential in "Song of Myself" Miller used sexual liberation as antinomian metaphor. Published in Paris, 1934, CANCER didn't appear in an American edition until 1960 when Miller was past 70. Whitman's poems were challenged by the district attorney of Boston but Miller's CANCER faced 50 obscenity charges resolved finally by the Supreme Court. One of the triggers of the Sixties.

Ezra Pound, an iconoclast far on the right of the political spectrum. Henry Miller, a Nietzchean nihilist with an anarchistic distrust of all institutions. Both romantics who cannot believe with Whitman in the dream of American possibility.

Whitman, Pound, Miller, all Voices Without Restraint. Crucial American influences on The Beat Generation.

The Beat Generation. In the next decade The Beat Generation will come to be recognized as the most important group of poets and writers in the history of America.

Jack Kerouac, spokesperson for The Beat Generation wrote a panoramic rhapsody infused with Whitman's identification with the common, the lowly, the downtrodden. Kerouac eulogizes his hoboes and wanderers in the same natural speech which caused James Russell Lowell to keep Whitman off the shelves at Harvard. Kerouac's prose line, his long, endlessly unpunctuated, surging sentences are based on Whitman's "Song of Myself" and like Whitman Kerouac is a celebrant who remains optimistic, despite all odds, despite all suffering struggle pain failure, he remains optimistic because he knows the journey is perpetual and has no end.

Kerouac's friend Allen Ginsberg is even closer to Whitman. "Howl," written exactly a century after "Song of Myself," uses the same long line. In Whitman's case as in Ginsberg's form becomes a function of the freedom to which the poet aspires. The holy, holy, holy, everything is holy is magnificent Whitman AH and AHA ecstasy.

Ginsberg is less ambivalent than Whitman about the human price we pay for commerce and industry, more in accord with Pound and Miller in his suspicion of Moloch, his cannibal dynamo of industry named after the Babylonian god to whom children were sacrificed. But Ginsberg's antinomianism has been, like Whitman's, the wound dresser, adhesive, sewing a communual purpose. So Ginsberg helped organize the peace

marchers in the Sixties, was witness to the Chicago National Convention in 1968, along with his friend William S. Burroughs, who may be the most antinomian of all The Beats.

Lawrence Ferlinghetti, who was arrested for publishing "Howl," Ferlinghetti, whose City Lights Books is antinomian mecca of the world, Ferlinghetti, whose A CONEY ISLAND OF THE MIND has sold more copies than any book of poetry by any living American poet, Ferlinghetti, antinomian to the end, sees the poet as enemy of the state.

JACK KEROUAC

TROPIC OF CANCER

BANNED!

Henry Miller

The antinomian legacy of Whitman, Pound, Miller, Kerouac, Ginsberg, Burroughs, Ferlinghetti, and so many other poets, writers, artists, musicians, filmmakers leads to our door and in this final moment having stood in the shadows for too long we step out and

now we stand on the

brink on the edge

at the ending of time

Time was Time is Time will be no more

and it's The Big Bang Epiphany

in the gap between thought and image

Voices streams racing

whispering through our blood

pleading through our bones

strange activities of our nerves

the unconscious life of our minds

a tetrameter of iambs marching

shouting Voices Without Restraint

Alchemically Transmutative Symbol Decipherment

The Book as Sacred Elixir

Manger du Livre Eat The Book

and The Word will set you free

Resurrection: photo by Carl Scharwath

The shortest distance between two points is creative distance

and Allen Ginsberg howls

"I saw the best minds of my generation destroyed by madness, starving, hysterical naked"

and Diane di Prima rants

"the only war that matters is the war against the imagination, all other wars are subsumed in

It"

and Amiri Baraka chants

"They have turned, and say that I am dying. That I have thrown my life away. They have left me alone, where there is no one, nothing, save who I am. Not a note nor a word."

And Lawrence Ferlinghetti paints PICTURES OF THE GONE WORLD

Allen Ginsberg Diane di Prima Amiri Baraka

Lawrence Ferlinghetti

Numinous howls and rants and chants and paintings

and years of tears come fiercely flowing streaming

all the pain wells up

years of failure of not being enough for anyone

years of wandering lost on the outside

Outlaw

being told "you ain't shit you don't fit what the

fuck you doin here? all you've done is create pain and sorrow wouldn't

you be better off dead?"

Turning away from walking away from disappearing from

Authorities the past

The Dead

in the hermetic corridors of authority The Dead

somberly splash in their shallow sewers

devouring and regurgitating themselves

and with tears in my eyes a snarl on my lips and peace in my heart I'm failing as no others dare fail

and I'm in the gap between thought and image

how'd I get here after all the years of not being self

after all the years of being Other

of floating out of my body on the ceiling

watching skin blood bones nerves going through the motions believing in space and time without realizing I was already Out out of sync

beyond chaos

breathing rhythms at the ending of time

and now here in the gap between thought and image

where the only distance is creative distance

Here Now at The Ending of Time

I focus all three eyes in wolf fashion

Closing Time

I walk through the stone called lump of fat

and I float through the fire that is central

and I enter the upper chamber of the golden pyramid

the confluence of all streams

polyglot commingling of all voices

Thalass feeds herself

and as I float over the open sarcophagus

I am

The Ocean of Consciousness

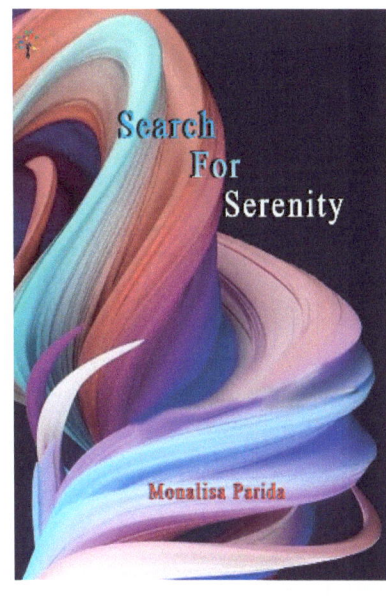

Knut Hamsun, progenitor of modernism, recipient of the 1920 Nobel Prize for Literature, in his 1890 essay, "On The Unconscious Life of The Mind," said "We would experience a little of the secret movements which are made unnoticed in the remote places of the soul, the capricious disorder of perceptions, the delicate life of fantasy held under the magnifying glass, the wanderings of these thoughts and feelings out of the blue: motionless, trackless journeys with the brain and heart, strange activities of the nerves, the whispering of the blood, the pleading of the bone, the entire unconscious life of the mind."

So what, so what is the ocean of consciousness?

"The only war that matters is the war against the imagination, all other wars are subsumed in it."

-Diane di Prima

The psychic makeup of creative persons attracts attention, but the actual artistic achievement is the bedrock of inquiry when it is directed toward understanding the artist, for the artistic disposition adheres to a charisma that attaches to the 'office' and has collective aspects.

"To be an artist is to fail, as no other dare fail."

-Samuel Beckett

Today Specialization is sold on every corner, fed in every home, brainwashed into every student, every young person. We are told that the only way to succeed here at the beginning of the 21st Century is to put all our time, energy, learning, and focus into one area, one field, one specialty (math, science, computer technology, business). If we don't we will fail. We are subtly and forcefully, implicitly and explicitly, encouraged to deny the rest of who we are, our total self, selves, our entire ever-changing being.

The postmodern brave new world resides inside the computer via The Web with only faint peripheral recognition to the person, the individual (and by extension the real global community), the real human being operating the machine. The idea of and belief in specialization as the only path, only possibility, has sped up the fragmentation, the alienation which began to grow rapidly within the individual, radically reshaping culture, a century ago with the birth of those Machiavellian revolutions in technology, industry, and war. And with the growing fracturing fragmentation and alienation comes the path - anger, fear, anxiety, angst, ennui, nihilism, depression, despair - that, for the person of action, leads to suicide. Unless, through our paradoxical leap of creative faith we engage ourselves in the belief, which can become a life mission, that regardless of the consequences, we can, through our engagement, our actions, our loving life work, make the world a better, safer, friendlier place in which to live. Sound naive?

What does this have to do with The Beat Generation, The Voice that, though trembling, speaks out against The Powers That Be, what place does this Outsider Poet Voice have in the real violent world in which we are immersed?

Are we too desensitized to the violence, to the fact that in the past Century alone we have murdered over 160 million people in one war after another, to even think it worthwhile to consider the possibility of a less violent world? Are we too small, too insignificant to make any kind of difference? The power-mongers have control. What difference can one little individual life possibly make possibly matter?

Today the X Y Z microserf millennial and why generations are swollen with young people yearning to express the creative energies buried in their hearts, seeping from every pore of their beings. They ache to change to heal the world.

Is it still possible? Is it too late? Is there anyone (a group? The Storm Generation?!) left to show the way to be an example? To be a guide? A mentor?

James Joyce, King of Modernism, said the idea of the hero was nothing but a damn lie that the primary motivating forces are passion and compassion. As late as 1984 people were laughing at George Orwell. Today, as we finally move into an AI artificial intelligence Orwellian culture of simulation life on the screen landscape, can we remember passion and compassion or has the postmodern ironic satiric death in life game laugh killed both sperm and egg?

Is there anywhere worth going from here?

Is it any wonder that today's youth have adopted Jack Kerouac, Allen Ginsberg, William S. Burroughs, Herbert Huncke, Gregory Corso, Neal Cassady, Lawrence Ferlinghetti, Amiri Baraka, Robert Creeley, David Amram, Diane di Prima, Ed Sanders, Anne Waldman, Bob Dylan, and all the other Beat Generation and related poets, writers, artists, musicians, photographers, filmmakers as their inspirational, life-affirming antinomian ancestors? These are people who have stood and still stand up against unreasoning power/right/might, looked that power in the eyes and said NO I don't agree with you and this is why. And they have spoken these words, not for money or for fame, but out of life's deepest convictions, out of the belief that we, each one of us, no matter our skin color our economic status our political religious sexual preferences, all of us have the right to live to dream as we choose rather than as some supposed higher moral authority prescribes for us.

In the next decade The Beats will come to be recognized as the most important group of poets and writers in the history of America. The Beats have given birth to new generations to new energies which are waking to the realization that the creative imagination provides salvation from suicide, from death in life, by revealing that there are alternative paths to explore in this world alternative paths that lead away from the mundane, the superficial, away from submission to mediocrity alternative paths opening into the inspired brilliant fire called LIFE.

The hallowed doors of Academia, Academia, which has become the bastion of conservative status quo thought, the doors of Academia are finally creaking open (just as it took so long for them to open to William Blake, Walt Whitman, James Joyce, Virginia Woolf, Samuel Beckett and all other original thinkers and expressionists) the doors are creaking open and, finally, at least a discourse on The Beats has begun.

"To be a poet, most of all to see."

–Henrik Ibsen

"I am more than my physical body and as such

I can see more than the physical world."

-Robert Monroe

produce produce produce

young people of all ages

let go your fears

embrace failure

take risks

be fearless

accept responsibility for your actions

for your successes and your failures

embrace failure

through failure you will know undreamed of success

If history is the embodiment of "fear, reason, social convention, and tradition" then it becomes the duty, the responsibility, the compelling creative urge of the Nabi, the Prophet, the Artist, the Poet to crack history's encrusted, iconostasic, shell releasing the dying and dead by invocation of The Word, pure thought, translated via pure energy into meaning full sound. The Poet, whose home is in Shadow in The Holy Unholy The Sacred and The Profane Realms of The Creative Imagination, as the synaptic link between spirit and matter, creates a new, enlightened awake being, awake world.

Out of the postmodern surreal chaos will evolve a structure, more vast than presently perceivable, that I call The Ocean of Consciousness. The structure is difficult to perceive because we are the structure. We are the synthesis. All streams of thought of con and unconsciousness flow to our Ocean of Consciousness, the structure that gives birth to, engulfs, encloses, creates, and expands the chaos.

Where do we, do I, begin and end? Do we begin? Do we end? The earth was once thought of as the center of the universe but our view, our perception, thrown out, into The Creative Imagination, expanded, and is now returning and we will soon see that We, each One of Us, are the center of a vast, interconnected, perhaps infinite, universe.

My quest to reach beyond Modernism and postmodernism to The Ocean of Consciousness may be partially defined as a literary scientific alchemical mysticism in which the mysterium tremendum is alive and doing well. It is a creative, numinous attempt to reach a Fourth Kingdom beyond but encompassing the alienated and alienating realms of spirit, matter, chaos, a Fourth Kingdom wherein lies the synthesis of apparently irreconcilable differences. The journey is inward, outward, centered, liminal, in the heart, and on the edge to silence, to the immaterial, psychological, emotional, mental, spiritual self, but also simultaneously to the spoken, visual, material, the world of action. But the emphasis of the journey is inward with self soul consciousness at heart.

Knowledge, from the inception of Modernism, and through postmodernism and Chaos to The Ocean of Consciousness, is reorganized, redefined through Literature, Art, Music, Photography, and Film. The genres are changing, the canons are exploding, as is culture. The mythopoetics, the privileged sense of sight, of modern, contemporary, avant-garde poets, musicians, artists, filmmakers are examples of art forms of a society, a culture, a civilization, a world in which humanity lives not securely in cities nor innocently in the country but on the apocalyptic, simultaneous edge of a new realm of being and understanding. The mythopoet, female and male, returns to the role of prophet-seer of shaman by creating myths that resonate in the minds the hearts of readers, myths that speak with the authority of the ancient myths, myths that are gifts from the shadow.

Ron Whitehead, U.S. National Beat Poet Laureate, with John Tytell

John Tytell is an American writer and academic He is professor emeritus of modern American literature at Queens College, City University of New York. Tytell's works on literary figures such as Jack Kerouac, Ezra Pound, Allen Ginsberg, Henry Miller, and William S. Burroughs have made him a leading scholar of the Beat Generation. He has written for the *American Scholar, Partisan Review, New York Times,* and *Vanity Fair.* His books include *Beat Transnationalism, Writing Beat and Other Occasions of Literary Mayhem, The Beat Interviews, Paradise Outlaws: Remembering the Beats, The Living Theatre: Art, Exile and Outrage, Passionate Lives: D.H. Lawrence, F. Scott Fitzgerald, Henry Miller, Dylan Thomas, Sylvia Plath—In Love, Ezra Pound: The Solitary Volcano, Naked Angels: Lives and Literature of the Beat Generation.*

When does the bullying in schools disappear?
Abdulloh Abdumominov writes on ending bullying in schools

- Uzebekistan

Sometimes I get frustrated when I see my peers or older boys than me. They ask their parents to bring them what they like, and they get it. But some parents refused their wish without understanding their child. In such a situation, they are understandable. After all, not all families are rich. Unfortunately, they are unaware that their child is under pressure from their school peers because that wish is not fulfilled. Our peers who are separated from their peers because of their headaches, cell phones, or the like become angry and depressed, both

at home and with their classmates. Scientists call such violence "bullying." We also have peers who have no idea that such pressure on others is a violation of legal equality. The most common situation is to hit each other with flaws. In such a situation, the child is proud of his parents. However, if a child cannot be proud of his peers behind his parents, he will be separated from others. Once I came across children who were discriminating against a blind child. I still regret not being able to say anything because they are older than me. Most people with disabilities are relatively talented. There are many examples of this. Children do not evaluate each other on this basis. So who is to blame for such tragedies? If a child is asked to bring something or is separated from others in class, it means that he or she has been harassed by peers. In such a situation, first of all, our parents and teachers should pay attention, be aware of the situation and establish friendly relations with children. Only then will the situation soften. It is important that we peers set an example for others, extend a helping hand to friends who are being persecuted.

SYNTHESIS OF HUMAN RIGHTS
Monalisa Parida

- India

Human Rights are rights inherent to all human beings, whatever our nationality, place of residence, sex, national or ethnic origin, colour, religion, language or any other status. We are all equally entitled to our human rights without discrimination. These rights are all interrelated, interdependent and indivisible.

"The violation of Human Rights is a temptation to which human spirit easily lends itself." (Heinrich Mann)

Human Rights violations have become very common nowadays. The Newspapers and T.V. tell us that every day and at every moment, somewhat in the world, Human Rights are being violated. The protection and preservation of Human Rights is a great challenge to every country in the world. Cases of violence, murder, rape, torture, child abuse, death due to starvation, death due to dowry, sexual harassment, custodial death have become rampant in the society.

"Violence against women is dearly not solved, not at all solved, and the reasons for it, which are controlling women's bodies in order to control reproduction, are definitely not solved." (Gloria Steinem)

The Human Rights of the people have been protected by "The Protection of Human Rights Act, 1993." It has been amended by protection of Human Rights (Amendment Act, 2006). In these ways we can also protect and support Human Rights for people around the world...............

- Know your rights

- Never give bribe

- Insist on your rights

- Educate the violators

- Be ready to commit your time

- Never let go when you are violated

- Expose the culprit and publish your encounter

- Challenge your violation in court

- Take pictures, voice or video recording to back up your claims

- Protect the right of others

- Never violate others

- Speak politely and softly, not forcefully with vulgar words

- Be right and stay upright

- Follow up till the end

- Educate everyone around you

A Yoruba proverb says, "olowo kan laa rin olosi mefa, olosi ni ohun na", meaning that a rich man among 6 poor people is also a poor man. This means that, an educated fellow in the midst of ignorant people is also an ignorant person. It is important that we educate everyone around us about human rights.

"India being a signatory to Universal Declaration of Human Rights, International covenant on Economic, Social and Cultural Rights and other international instruments, is legally as well as morally committed to ensure basic human rights to all its citizens and enact laws accordingly."

According to a statement made by Mr. J.S.Verma, the former chairman of the NHRC on Jan .15.o2003, just a few days before his demitting the office:

"It is often the state which is violator of Human Rights in maximum cases in the country. But the maximum responsibility to protect and safeguard the rights of its citizens also lies with the State."

It is the people; it is the duty of every individual to change their mentality. This can be brought about only through general awakening which make everyone understand the eternal values of life and dignity of an individual irrespective of caste, creed or sex. In the words of Swami Vivekananda that the "Self in you is the Self everywhere. "

"It has always been a mystery to me how men can feel honoured by the humiliation of their fellow beings."   (Mahatma Gandhi)

Monalisa Parida is from India, Odisha. She is a post graduate in English literature and a prolific poetess. She's very active in social media platforms and her poems have also been published in various e-journals and translated into different languages.

The Spring Day
short story by Sherzod Artikov

The reason for my three-year-old son's caprice was that there was no hot bread on the morning table. My attempts to calm the baby were in vain: he protested even more, and his whining grew into a loud cry. Then he began throwing pieces of bread on the table, which he was offered.

"Get that stubborn man out of my sight! " at one moment shouted angrily my father, who had been watching us in silence, frowning his eyebrows.

Not expecting such a reaction from my father, I froze for a moment. Then, without paying attention to me, I began to put pieces of cake in one pile and in turn kissed and brought them to the forehead.

"Take your son and leave the room! Now!" now my dad collected crumbs of bread from the table in the palm of his hand.

The little one, who had never seen grandfather so formidable before, cried out completely. And indeed, my father was always discreet and courteous. I took my son into my arms and headed for the door.

From an offense and anger I started shaking, and already in doors I said:

"Daddy, he is still a child. Quite small... Think about it, I was naughty. And so sometimes it is possible to get out of the house to see you, and you..."

The father kept silent, instead he brought bread crumbs to his mouth and swallowed them, drinking tea at the end.

With displeasure I went to another room, where I hugged a pillow and cried bitterly. And so I lay until my mother, brother and sister-in-law came to call me for lunch. No matter how much they begged and begged, I was adamant. Hugging my son, without saying a word, I looked somewhere far away. When the child fell asleep, my father appeared at the door. He held a plate with food in one hand and a cake in the other.

"Daughter, you have to eat on time, or you will ruin your stomach."

Having said that, he laid his handkerchief on the floor and carefully put bread and food.

"And then you may have a stomach ulcer. You know, there is no worse disease than this. It can be very painful."

I noticed how his strong hands, entangled with bloated veins, trembled. Deep wrinkles made his face look even more beautiful. For a moment, my father shifted his tired look to me. Seeing my determined mood, he took a deep breath and sat down in a chair in the corner of the room.

"It's Sunday," he said, sadly and looked towards the flowering apricot tree, and in my opinion, revived a little. "It's a spring Sunday! Spring has come! Warm days have come, the tree has begun to blossom. April in the yard. Mother Nature will unfold in all its glory. The charming smell of spring fills every cell of our bodies..."

And then he rested his one hand on the window sill, the second opened the window sash. And I still sat silently and motionlessly, demonstrating my resentment. I stroked the fluffy hair of my sleeping son in order not to look at my father.

"And during the war, spring was the same," my father continued, thoughtfully wiping his palms. "Spring awakening of nature blunted the horror of the war, helped to survive, to forget the reality, to endure what was happening around. At such moments shots from a happy childhood came up: here I am among my beloved parents, my sister, who was destined to live only four years. I can clearly see my father's intelligent face, kind mother with her beautiful black scythe. But a hail of bullets and projectiles, shattering us, a heavy landing of caterpillars, shrill squeals of flying airplanes brought me back to reality. And then I wanted to run out of the trench and shout loudly: "Why do we spill each other's blood? Why does this happen?!"

A bitter lump in my throat was choking me all the time trying to get out with a loud scream. At the same time, I could not express my thoughts, ask questions that tormented me. The realization that you are shooting at a completely alien person who has not caused you anything bad was painful and tormenting.

At such moments German guys – Karl, Sebastian, Paul stood before my eyes at one side, and I with my comrades on the other. Why do we kill each other? Because before the war I lived in Margilan, and they lived in Munich or Dresden. There was no end to my thinking..."

Daddy first started talking about the war. And before, we talked to him very often on different topics, but he always tried to avoid this one. Papa got a family, children very late in life. When I was born, he was over fifty years old, so my brother and I became a light in the window: he literally trembled at us, cherished in every way.

On warm spring and summer evenings after work, Daddy used to put us on his bike and ride around the city. Then we would sit on a bench in front of the fountain and enjoy our favorite chocolate ice cream. And then Daddy told us interesting stories from his life, and even then not a word about the war. When my brother or I were interested in his military exploits, he immediately changed the topic.

"...In Ukraine, not far from Lviv, our company was captured. On the train on the way to Poland, I did not leave the painful reflections and thoughts. We were taken to the outskirts of Krakow to the Auschwitz concentration camp – the most terrible and scary place in the world. The Germans called it Auschwitz, the local population – "death camp".

The camp was divided into three settlements. Together with other prisoners, I was taken to the second ward. More and more prisoners entered the camp every day and were divided into four groups by the Germans. The first group included all those who were found unfit for work: first of all the sick, the deep old, the disabled, children, elderly women and men, who also arrived in bad health, of medium height or weak physique. Poor people immediately went to the gas chambers, where they found a terrible, painful death. Then their bodies were burned in crematoriums. In the second group, healthy, strong prisoners were selected for the hardest slave labor in the industrial enterprises around the concentration camp. The third group included twins, dwarves, people with unnatural physical characteristics, who then went to various medical experiments with the doctors of the Third Reich. The fourth group, mostly beautiful women, were selected for personal use by the Germans as servants or given over to the laundries and canteens of military units.

As part of the second group, I was sent to work in heavy industry, which was half an hour from the concentration camp. Spare parts for tanks were produced at the factory, so the work was extremely heavy and harmful. The premises were so stuffy that by the middle of the day the prisoners became incapacitated. All day long, like slaves, we had to listen to the severe insults of the German guards and tolerate their whipping. We were fed with broth of potato peel and stale black bread.

In the evening, on the way to the barracks, many impoverished prisoners were lying down with fatigue, and then the annoyed Germans simply shot them. Someone gathered all courage and strength and reached the brick buildings, but on the way up to the next floor he lost consciousness. He also followed his comrades to the other world.

We worked even on Sundays. Here, life and death went hand in hand. When machines failed or were to be repaired, we, the prisoners, were forced to have a day off, which was in the spring and summer months. On such days, we were taken to a large square surrounded by a wire fence and kept under the open sky, be it rain, hail, or the unbearable heat.

In our part of the camp there were four gas chambers and as many crematoriums. On weekends, we often watched the prisoners being led into these cells. Among them, we could see very young ones. Everyone knew that after some time they would be burned alive. While our clouded consciousnesses were trying to digest the situation, a monstrous smell was coming out of the crematorium chimneys, from which we were all turned away. And there were more and more ashes of the dead near the crematorium, and they eventually turned into a whole mountain. Prisoners brought to work in crematoriums, one after another, took into their cars what was left of the poor people. It is painfully bitter to realize that only recently they were alive and steadfast in their imminent death.

Once, if I am not mistaken, in April of 1944, on another day off we were dragged to the site. The prisoners, exhausted by hunger and difficult conditions, resembled living corpses: they gathered in one place with difficulty while moving. The prisoners were seized by fear, because it was Easter. Everyone knew that on the festive days, the Germans entertained themselves in every way, mocking the prisoners.

For example, they organized running competitions: the first one who reached the finish line remained alive, and the other three were immediately waiting to die from a hail of bullets. If they wanted to listen to the song, they ordered several prisoners to stand in formation along the wire fence. One acted as a soloist, others sang with the choir. Woe performers were forced to sing songs praising the Nazis. The worst thing was when the prisoners were forced to run back and forth with their right hand raised, with a loud cry "Heil Hitler!", which gave them a great pleasure. Especially this "entertainment game" was widely used when Jews were led into gas chambers. The prisoners, raising their right hands high without taking a breath, had to greet the leader of the Nazis and escort the doomed into the arms of death. If someone did not do it properly, he would follow the Jews to the gas chamber.

But this time the guards seemed serious. There was no trace of the festive mood, and in the faces of these brutal guards unbridled vigilance and caution were reflected. It also turned out to be suspicious that the commandant

himself was carrying out the inspection. The SS men, with automatic rifles in their hands, stood humbly beside the wire fence. From afar, a black car appeared. At the sound of the approaching vehicle, the commandant and his assistants ran out of his block and lined up in a row.

The car stopped right in front of us. Because of the rain that did not stop all night, it was covered with mud and clay.

"Heil Hitler!" the commandant and soldiers greeted the guest in one voice.

The military official greeted everyone and began to look around. He was tired and looking sadly at the ash mountain near the crematorium, at the gray and horrible barracks. Then, he approached the wire fence and began to watch the prisoners.

He was a broad-shouldered, statuesque man of forty-five to fifty years old. Accidentally, his gaze fell on my side and he called me to his place with gestures. Here, an interpreter approached the chief.

"Are you Jewish? " the officer asked, looking at me from head to toe.

The young interpreter translated every word he said.

"No, an Uzbek..." I answered without raising my head.

"Do you see the car?" he pointed at his car.

"Yes, I did..."

"In half an hour you have to clean the car. The time has been going by..."

The first time I did not hear his instructions, only after the second explanation I nodded my head as a sign of consent. The driver of the car and one SS man brought a bucket of water, a rag, and I settled down to work.

For the first time in my life, I stood beside such a progress of technique, watched it with my own eyes and touched with my hands. Before that, I only looked at them in photo cards. My father had a well-known caravanserai in the district. There I had to meet a Kokand arba and phaetons of Russian officers. During the collectivization, it was taken away from my father and then I never saw anything like this again. And here in front of me is a real car – black, shiny, with a soft seat and a lot of devices. Behind the body I could see the name "Mercedes".

Despite the exhausted strength and fainting, I wiped the car shiny. Having finished my work, I returned to the ranks of prisoners. I sat down on the ground and leaned on a wire fence, and breathed. The chief, accompanied by the commandant, left the building and started checking my work. He circled the car, walked around the body with his index finger and was satisfied. Then he shouted something out to the commandant, who in turn gave instructions to the soldier standing nearby.

Meanwhile, the chief, leaning against the body of the car, smoked. Soon, a soldier appeared, holding a whole plate of white fresh bread. The chief together with him approached the fence and called me. When I came to him, he patted me on my bony shoulder and said that the contents of the plate were now mine. There were slices of white bread in the saucer, the smell of which made my heart beat faster and I almost lost consciousness. After hugging the food, I hurried back. Seeing five dozen eyes, I felt uncomfortable. At that moment I wanted to close my eyes and eat delicious bread, but my conscience did not allow me to act selfishly.

"Take, Umar!" I first approached my Tashkent friend. He did not immediately dare to stretch out his hand, but after the second time I offered the bread to him, he broke off a piece and put it in his mouth. And he returned the remaining half on the saucer.

"Look, what bread!" I said when I approached a young boy from Tajikistan. "Naufal, try it."

He also took only half of the slice. The rest of the prisoners did the same. The last slice was given to a Kazakh comrade. When I returned an empty plate to the soldier, the chief came to me:

"Are you crazy?" he said nervously. "It was a reward for your clean work. Instead of satisfying hunger yourself, you gave everything to the last crumb to others. Why did you do this?"

Before my eyes, like a film, flashed a young wife of Umar Islambekov, who had children before our captivity, the old mother of Naufal, Niyazov's father, who lost one leg, and many others.

"Why did you do this? "he repeated his question.

"Because in the Homeland their native, favorite people are waiting for them... And nobody is waiting for me... " my voice trembled.

Having heard my answer, the officer took a deep breath. And then I looked into his eyes. In his tired look, I could see something else, human. For a moment he thought, then threw a cigarette and looked around. With sorrow, he looked at the crematorium, at the ashes mountain, and said: "Got vergib uns, wir sind alle Geschöpfe".

After giving instructions to the commandant, he headed for the car. On the way he looked in my direction and whispered something to the interpreter. When the black car disappeared from view, the SS man led me, on the instructions of the interpreter, I did not know where. At these moments, as if feeling guilty in front of me, my friends pressed harder and harder against the wire fence. Their eyes full of pity and despair accompanied me towards the imminent death.

"Islambekov, Chariev, Niyazov ... My friends, do not remember me wistfully ..."

As we walked, my whole life flashed before my eyes. Mom, dad, sister... Our house... The garden with the duck trees...

But the thought that there was no one to mourn me helped to accept death. On the way, everything whispered a prayer that I learned as a child. But somehow the soldier took me to the dining room. I followed him silently, then he ordered me to sit down at the table. Very soon, the cook brought food on the tray: a few slices of white bread, steak and apricot juice. While I was digesting what was happening, the interpreter was sitting in front of me.

"The Brigadeführer ordered me to feed you. That you sit, eat... "

With trembling hands I lifted a spoon. The translator, having taken out a notebook from his pocket, began to consider a small photo of some woman.

"Tasty bread?" he asked with a smile.

In response, I nodded my head. With shaking lips, I broke the bread and started to eat meat. Immediately, I felt a burst of energy.

"Do not be shy about it. Eat it, you're welcome – it is already lunch time. And your friends will soon be fed. From today on, you will be properly fed. Instead of boiled potato peel, you will eat potatoes in uniform. This is an order of the Brigadeführer."

Having put the spoon on the dish, I shifted my astonished gaze to it for a moment. He, not paying attention to this, cheerfully asked:

"What is your name?"

For the first time, I could see the translator so close. He was the same age as me, about twenty-five years old. He was a nice, kind guy.
"My name is Odil," I answered.

"And me – Richard. I taught Russian at the Berlin University. Unfortunately, I was not able to finish it. In 1938, I was drafted into the army and remained there in the war."

Richard was still with me for a little while, got up and headed for the door. Turning back, he looked at me, then at the still life hanging on the wall.

"Very soon your troops will reach these places as well. There is not much left ... It will be over soon."

Nine months later, at the end of January 1945, a Soviet army liberated the Auschwitz concentration camp. Umar Islambekov did not see the day, shortly before he died of typhoid. But he was very young, he married at the age of 18 and left for the front at 19. Naufal hanged himself in the deep autumn. And how many of my friends and comrades could not withstand the harsh life of a concentration camp, and this terrible place was their last refuge. Only me, Niyazov and a few more managed to survive in the death camp.

...Many years have passed since then, but those days are still alive in my memory. Especially on such spring days I remember that magical Sunday of 1944, the story of white bread, when those happy faces of the prisoners who tasted a piece of the most delicious delicacy stand before my eyes. I remember my enemies – Brigadier and interpreter Richard, who in spite of everything, showed mercy and compassion. Perhaps among them were the same ones, who did not find answers to many questions that tormented them. And seeing so much blood, death and conscience around them, they still woke up in their stale souls. This explains the action of that officer.

Daddy was silent. Finally, I got up and went to the window. The room became cool, so I shut the window. Standing there for a while, I got closer to my father. I wanted to say something to him. He was looking somewhere far away, his hands clinging to the handle of the chair were shaking.

"Daddy, forgive me..." I rushed into his arms.

I cried, Daddy cried too.

"You know... you know, my daughter... every piece of bread, every little one means a lot to me. I still want to share my bread with them..."

Definitions:

*Got vergib uns, wir sind alle Geschöpfe – God have mercy on us, animals that have lost their human form.

**Brigadeführer – a special rank of senior officials of the SS, corresponding to the army rank of major general.

Sherzod Artikov was born in 1985 in the city of Marghilan of Uzbekistan. He graduated from Fergana Polytechnic institute in 2005. He was one of the winners of the national literary contest "My Pearl Region " in the direction of prose in 2019. In 2020, his first authorship book " The Autumn's Symphony " was published in Uzbekistan by publishing house "Yangi Asr Avlodi" . In 2021, his works were published in the anthology books called "World Writers" in Bangladesh, "Asia sings" and "Mediterranean Waves " in Egypt, "Emerging horizons" in India, " Healing through verses" in Canada in English language and his authorship book " The autumn's symphony" was published in Spanish and English in Cuba by Argos Iberoamericana Publishing House.

Translated into English by the author

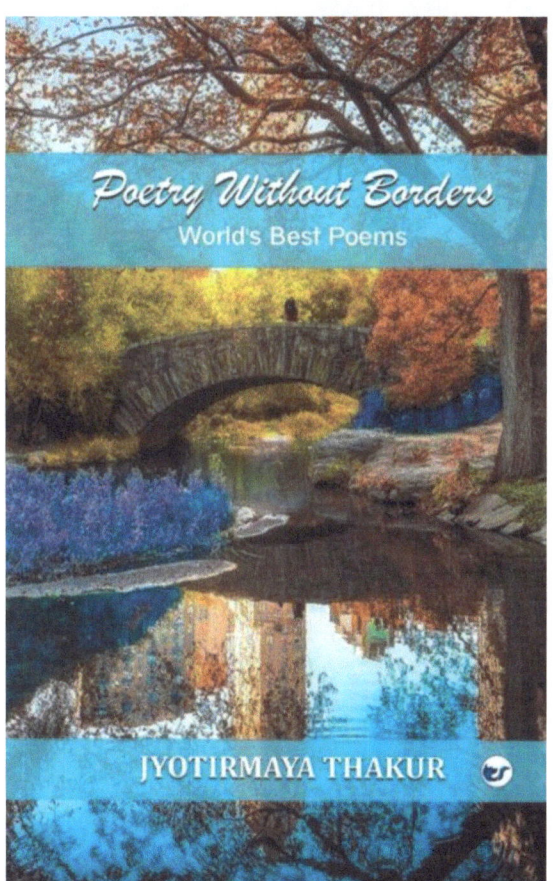

A GRIFFIN'S WORK: THE LIVING TREASURE

- Joe Kidd

grim sloven creature at the edge of the mote
slow and hungry, self indulged
an easier target, could never attempt

my love for life, my ravishing mate
round black eyes on each side of her head
long shimmering wings, curved and smooth

this day will end when the crickets chirp
until then the little ones keeping warm
away from light, away from sight

that circling shadow, a menacing entrant
but no match for a sentinel fast and fierce
nothing blue, nothing gray, shall imperil this day

we arrived with the wind on the equinox
birth and rebirth, nature born again
in a nest of danger, a building sanctified

break free from the shell in which you find comfort
curiosity, courage, and innocent freedom
emerge to a realm of merciless beauty

that one must die to feed another
I pledge that today it is not our fate
but to defend at cost a raging future

beckoning souls unseen and unknown
recognized, in a silent warning
the necessity of relentless motion

save us now, we can wait no longer
for your light to shine upon this hill
and carry us gently on feathered wings

Joe Kidd is a working, published poet and songwriter touring North America and Western Europe. In 2020, he published *The Invisible Waterhole*, a collection of spiritual and sensual verse. He has been awarded by the Michigan Governor's Office and the US House of Representatives for his work to advance Peace, Social Justice, and Cultural Diversity. Joe is a member of National & International Beat Poet Foundation (USA), Angora Poets (Paris France), and 100,000 Poets For Change International.

www.joekiddandsheilaburke.com

Monsif Beroual was born in MIDELT, Morocco, on 1994. He graduated from Sidi Mohammed Ben Abdlalah University, section Public Law at Taza City, Morocco. He is a multi- awarded: (MEDITERRANEAN POETRY PRIZE 2020/2021, Rome-Italy. PENTASI B Spring Torch of Poetry, 2017, India. Pablo Neruda Medal 2017, Rabat-Italy. PENTASI B Universal Inspirational Poet 2016, Ghana.) and International renowned poet. His poems have been translated into a dozen languages : Spanish , French , Chinese , Polish , Arabic , Romanian, Bulgarian, Bangla, Serbian, Croatian, Italian, and Taiwanese. His poems have been published in several International magazines, in more than 300 international anthologies and magazines. He is a young fellow with BIG vision of sharing Love and Peace in the World. He feels that humanity and all creatures have the right to live peacefully and be treated with compassion, respect and love which are visible in his writings.

The Heart of a P.O.E.T.

– Monsif Beroual

In this humanity sake journey

I'll be like Jean Piaget

when he starts seeing the world

through a child's heart

or like Alexis Tocqueville

when he decides

to walk in this endless road

to reach American Democracy

or like Charles Wright Mills, who established the politics of

truth through the promise

to be honest and pure no matter how will be the cost,

 and like Spinoza who takes the magic stare from the universe

to unchain a hidden truth

or like Friedrich Nietzsche

when he screamed loud: " Zardach, god is dead!"

when he discovered the world is getting colder.

and I wished over all ends or start within philosophy's heart may our world be embraced

by love song again.

Bazaar

- Tapeshwar Amef

I don't know, how

have I taken

the roots

Under the earth -

Unbecoming of my darkness.

Is that how

Flowers bloom

Petaled,

upon the land bazaar

Merchandise of the sky

Profundity photo by Carl Scharwath

Perhaps Someday, I Will Find A Word To Mourn My Dead One's Death.

- John Chinaka Onyeche

Rememberajc.wordpress.com

That of my father's disappearance in my hometown like the widow's last coins lost. Maybe I should coin out a word, or I am yet to learn a metaphor with which I would mourn him better with after the many years of his name that danced in the East-wind silently as a forgotten song. Or maybe, I should birth for him a lexicon from where his voice, that which went silent in the year 2013 will come back and retell the stories of his life as a father. It is just like what looks as outside his, but what it is, is that which is called brotherly hatred in the care-given undertone and my father walked into the obliviousness of the world; no return as what we used to know him for. Or should I forget about her, she whom I find comfort in her eyes, her voice and her love for an offspring echoes; Janet. She was love in everything she does till that fateful morning when the day became darkened, eyes red as it rained rivers as if, if I cry oceans, maybe the deads will be brought back to life again. She laid down on that bed, pointing to these pictures of Christ Jesus on the walls healing the sick, and she whispered to me; "son, know thy God and creator, for it is as a duty even as you are becoming a father after your siblings". It was as with a voice muffled in pain in an emptied room she murmured those words to my ears; "son, go to the school, get your result and return so we could discuss the future". But I came back meeting with a white casket, people gathered in tears and they all echoed in unison, here comes her son who will decide where his mother's remain shall be laid to rest out of this troubled world. This was how I lost my parents when they were yet to tell me about the future, of how to become a man. And the ocean emptied on the rooftop of my grandfather without a remnant. Perhaps, someday I would find a metaphor to carve out their space in the tablet of time and memory.

John Chinaka Onyeche "Rememberajc" (he/his) is a husband, father and a poet from Nigeria. He writes from the city of Port Harcourt Rivers State, Nigeria. He is currently a student of History and Diplomatic Studies at Ignatius Ajuru University Of Education Port Harcourt Rivers State.

A Butterfly on Stage
Short Drama by Bogdana Găgeanu

Characters:

Fiona: a girl born with no hands, who dreams to become an actress

Paul :the director of a big theatre company

Gelda: Fiona's mother

Matthew, an actor of the big theatre company

Act 1

Everything is happening in London, a city with many theatre companies. Fiona has a big dream: to become an actress. But she was born without hands. Still, she is pursuing her dream and fights with the system.

Scene 1

Gelda:-Sweetheart, I found an announcement about a casting at a big theatre company. Would you like to try? I know it is your big dream to become an actress.

Fiona(enthusiastic): -Yes, mom. When is the casting?

Gelda: Tomorrow. But I don't know if you have enough time to prepare yourself.

Fiona:-Don't worry. I'll do my best.

Gelda (a little sad):-I am afraid that maybe you will be disappointed. You know...There are only beautiful actresses ...

Fiona:-Mom, it's not the beauty that counts on a stage, but the emotion.

Gelda:-Ok. We will go.

Scene 2
The day of the audition

Fiona and her mother, Gelda, come together at the theatre company. There stands Paul, the director of the company.

Fiona: Hi,I have come for the audition.
Paul: Sure. Is the lady here too for the audition?
Gelda: Oh, no. I am her mother. I can wait outside.
Paul:-Come with me, young lady.
Paul and Fiona go in the audition room.
Paul:-This is Matthew, your partner for the audition. He is one of our best actors in the company.
Fiona:*(happy)*-Nice to meet you.
Matthew:-Me, too.
Paul: Let's begin. Fiona, say the lines, please.
Fiona.-Sure. *(She is concentrating)*."I was a butterfly but I did not know I was a butterfly until I met you. Then, I began to fly."
Matthew:-Wow! You are so talented!
Paul*(aggressive)*: I decide who is talented here. You can do something with your hands, Fiona. Like imitating some wings of a butterfly.
Fiona: I can't. I was born without hands. Look! (She takes away her jacket)
Paul: Then, You can't become an actress. Please, get out!
Fiona *(crying)*: Why? Just because I don't have hands? Theatre is about emotion.
Paul: Get out!
Matthew: Give her a chance!
Paul: Get out too! You're fired!

Act 2

Scene 1
Fiona and Matthew leave the company.
Gelda is shocked.
Fiona is in tears.

Fiona: -I don't want to become an actress. I am a loser. Matthew was fired because of me.
Matthew:-That is not true. I trust you. We will play together.
Fiona:-How?
Matthew--You will see. We will go to my place, record the play and put it on a Youtube Channel and on Facebook. People will watch us and maybe we will have the chance that a director will see our talent and hire us.
Fiona: Ok, mom, come with us.

Scene 2

In Matthew's house.

Gelda is helping the two to record the play. Matthew and Fiona are dressed properly, with make-up on their face.
They say the lines. Matthew ends it with his last line:

Matthew *(emotionally)*:-"I love you, my butterfly. I am your flower. I will wait you every day, as long as I live."

Fiona *(applauds)*:-Bravo! You are great! I recorded and I put everything on Youtube.

Scene 3

Fiona (happy): Wow! A lot of people watched our video! I owe you everything, Matthew. My lines are true. I can fly because of you.

Matthew -You are a butterfly on stage. You don't have hands, you have wings.

Fiona(sad): A director gave us a message. He wants us for his company. Do you think he saw that I have no hands?

Matthew:-Yes. But he searched the emotion in you. The public is conquered by your love and commitment.

Gelda:-Congratulations! Let's fly and spread our colours!!!!

School of Arts and Poetry

Certificate of Excellence

Drama Contest, June 2021

Painting by Maki Starfield

ME FIVE YEARS LATER
- dedicated to Rothko

Maki Starfield

Five years later, I sometimes think about something like this. Trying to paint a picture like Rothko.

I'm too busy with my daily life right now. I want to escape as soon as possible, color various human emotions like Rothko, and develop infinite time and space. How happy it would be to go on a journey to one's own inner world, away from all social customs and ties!

No financial anxiety, becoming free from relationships with family and surroundings... Like Rothko, I want to paint with my room as a motif. Neither for myself, nor for someone else, but only for the love of God.

Will such a spiritual composure be born? Somehow, while predicting the future, maybe my life will be cornered by something.

I don't really love Rothko's paintings, but I'm attracted to Rothko's soul, which can produce such colors.

Let the past, present, and future live together in one canvas and trip us away to a world of nothingness. You can experience the crazy and ecstatic feeling that comes from his paintings! Isn't it happy to go from a mundane time to a completely different flow of time even for a moment?

Within Rothko's and my shared subconscious, a common consciousness seems to coexist. This common consciousness is the vibration of cosmic consciousness.

If I had the same karma as Rothko, I might be able to paint like him. Without it, it would be difficult. However, because there is a connection between our souls my heart is attracted.

We live in material time. Behind the scenes, there is also the time of existence after death. I admire Rothko's paintings, which bring the myriad visions that occur in this after-death time to this world.

DREAM-LIKE LIBRARY

Trishna Basak

After reaching somewhere

Our life as if, becomes a book,

Someone sees just by turning the leaves,

Someone just reads one or two pages,

And amid all these remains alive a

Dream-like library!

All of us can't reach that library,

While somebody can

And Those who can, they stand

Straight with erect spine

Like an endless milkyway in the bookshelf

And awaiting their intimate readers.

On reaching somewhere

The life of some of us

Turns into a refulgent library.

(Translated by Ujjal Ghosh)

Maki Starfield, a poet, a translator and a painter, born in Ehime, 1972. She earned her Master of Arts from Sophia University, getting the diploma of International business management and the certificate of TESOL in Canada. She is a representative in Japan of Immagine Poesia, a member of Japan Universal Poets Association, and Japanese haiku associates. She has been honored with the following: Guido Gozzano Prize (Honorable Mention) 2018,2019; Naji Naaman Literary Prize (Creativity) 2020; Pushcart prize nomination 2020; and, Sahitto International Award for Literature 2021.

Woodstock and the Man on the Moon

Timely Short Fiction by Larry Jaffe

It was the summer of 69, man first walked on the moon and Woodstock was an alien nation. The Vietnam War had stricken both nations – napalm stripped the jungles, denuded a country and America's children rebelled. A country that once stood for all that was good was infected with greed from the inside out. The military industrial complex was out to win the world and as the Beverly Hillbillies stated they struck black gold – oil. It was all about oil and drugs and as American forces took losses in a land they never loved, the United States was raped by its own bureaucrats pretending to be statesmen and the bold. There were no wandering moments; the U.S. right to intervene was invoked to protect corporate interests but not its people. America right or wrong, America love it or leave it was the patriot's call. America was left to clean up France's handiwork to protect the coffers of Mr. Brown, Mr. Root, Mr. Shell and Mr. Standard, oil companies all.

But there was revelry in the streets as well. It was a new age – the so-called Age of Aquarius was born during these hectic times. Emerging from the chaos was a new form of citizen, one that championed the underdog and sought to make right the wrongs of a government gone haywire. It was like there were two governing bodies – one that wore the innocent faces of the do-gooders and a shadowy entity pulling the strings of the establishment to the song of the greed and avarice.

And then the children screamed out. It was the first blooming of baby boomers. And they shouted from rooftops and parks, "Peace Now!" But the nation did not listen and peace became more violent.

It was 1969, they were putting a man on the moon, shredding a civilization in Asia, but it was the Summer of Love and the participants regaled.

Scott Spector fell in love yet again. It was the third time that summer and it seemed as if he would fall in love every other day, so strong was the urge to procreate or get laid. He was at the tender age of 21, the cusp of manhood and was on his own in the wilds of New York City in the jungle of Manhattan an area known as the Lower East Side. Unfortunately, for Scott, his loves lasted less than 24 hours.

Seeing through Scott's eyes was a world gone awry. As the first branch of baby boomers to take on the world, they thought they could do anything including stopping a war. They marched on Washington as if they owned it – millions of them shouting trick slogans and raising hands unified in peace signs.

It was the counterculture, the mischievous misfits, and Scott was once told he was part of the unwashed and unwanted although he bathed daily and had many friends. There was an aura around the time, a sense of comradery between folks that he never experienced before. There really was love in the air and from his point of view, the world seemed to be moving into a kinder, gentler age – it really felt as if there was an Age of Aquarius as the song suggested.

Scott felt so naïve yet undefeatable in spirit. He had yet to hit the age of attrition. Scott had dropped out of school because it did not meet his artistic temperament. He avoided the draft because of chronically bad knees and could not hold up under jungle assault. It was Vietnam and drugs and rock and roll and he wanted to be in love. After all, it was the summer of love.

Scott's apartment was on the Lower East Side of Manhattan. This was not a good place to live. It was not gentrified like today. It was nasty, full of crime and tenements. The streets were littered with abandoned mattresses and other what not. He never understood the plethora of mattresses curbside. Where did the people sleep if their mattresses were in the gutter? For a brief second he wondered if people slept on streets. It was a hot summer.

Scott lived with three friends Ralph, his girl Shulie and Jerry. They inhabited a four story walkup and were on the second floor. It was a big flat with 3 bedrooms, one toilet but the bathtub was in the kitchen and a plethora of varmints.

The rats and roaches were abated through a unique method called "feeding the frenzy." They pried up a loose floorboard and discarded various food scraps to the denizens below. It appeared to work. The wake up in the middle of the night nibbling on body parts seemed to subside.

Jerry was on a macrobiotic stint and refused to eat anything but brown rice. Trouble was he could not cook a lick and the brown rice concoction he was always formulating was inedible. This led to the various excuses he put forth when Scott caught him one day devouring a Nathan's hotdog. At first he looked rather guilty, but then relaxed and furtively explained his reasoning.

"You see Scott, spiritually I am macrobiotic, but on this plane at this time it is not a practical choice so I can substitute hotdogs for brown rice. As long as I maintain my spiritual self macrobioticly, it is all good."

Scott looked on with a quizzical expression, somehow hotdogs and brown rice did not go together. Jerry continued with his rant.

"I only eat Nathan's because of their history. It is a people's food."

Folding his arms over his chest he looked positively radiant with his explanation – a Jewish Buddha if you will.

Scott nodded his head not wanting to tell him his true thoughts; that he was basically full of it but told a good story. They were friends and he had no desire to antagonize him by telling him that the road to Nirvana was littered with hotdog stands. Perhaps he thought that Nathans was closer to God than the Sabretts stand on the corner. Even on his deathbed he steadily maintained his allegiance to macrobiotic land. The Twinkies under his bed would have disagreed but who was Scott to tell a friend he was full of it.

The love in the apartment was well centered for its time. The roommates loved each other as friends, but that was where it stopped. Obviously Ralph and Shulie were hitting it off in more ways than one, even Jerry had an uptown girlfriend who they never saw but supposedly existed, but might have been part of his macrobiotic diet. He talked of her all the time, how hip and artistic she was. Ralph and Shulie thought she was probably a librarian. Nevertheless, Scott was the only one who flitted from love to love. He did not understand why he could just not settle down with one human being and be happy.

Truth be told it bothered him. He once again called his friend Teresa angsting away for the umpteenth time that month. Teresa was his roaming partner a real buddy and not a love interest there. They just pal-ed around together and once stayed up all night just to see the sunrise in Central Park and then subwayed downtown to Little Italy to feast on freshly made bread and coffee.

"Hey Teresa, it's me Scott."

"No shit Sherlock, you only call me every day, you would think by now I just might recognize your voice."

Sheepishly, he replied, "Sorry T, just going through a bad time, ya know?"

"Whenever I talk to you lately it's because you are going through bad times. Just once I would love you to call me when things are good. You need to grow up and get your act together. I don't want to hear about it anymore." She slammed down the phone.

Scott left the phone booth forlorn. He went for a walk, figured he might fall in love again looking at the pretty women in the village. But that seemed too shallow for a change. He walked and walked and walked some more. He stopped at Café Figaro at the corner of Bleeker and McDougal Streets – the heart of the village. It was crowded as usual; he found a table outside in a distant corner. Absent-mindedly he picked at the tablecloth. Scott did not want to feel sorry for himself, but something inside just felt broken. He looked around the room and people were talking and laughing, smoking cigarettes and drinking coffee. Scott felt so alone. He thought about his conversation with Teresa, Sister T as he called her. She was more like a sister to him than his own family. He could open up and tell her anything and she would listen, really listen. Now he had lost her. Maybe he opened up too much, told her too much. He could feel tears forming at the corners of his eyes.

He struggled a smile to the waitress and ordered an iced chocolate one of his favorite drinks. The waitress, a jaunty sort, flirted with him wordlessly when she brought his drink. It made him smile a little more. He wondered about his life so far. Nothing special, he just thought in generalities, wondering this and wondering that.

"I need a break, I need a real girlfriend," he thought to himself. But then caught himself in what had become a cycle of ruts. "I just need to get my life together like Sister T said. No more looking for lost loves even in the right places."

Scott had been writing since he was 8 years old and always had hopes of writing that great American Novel. Now he thought he would settle for a short story, great or not, just write something – finish something – thinking of the unfinished manuscripts in his room. He was reading the Village Voice and noticed as usual that there were not many want ads for writers. In fact, he never ever saw one. Plenty of ads for salesmen though. Then he saw it:

Writers wanted for antiestablishment rock magazine.

Scott left Figaro and rapidly walked home. He did not look at all the girls or stopped to browse shop windows. He was a man on a mission. He was excited. Scott had stopped by a phone booth and called the number, spoke to the publisher some guy named Romeo Hudson and they just clicked on the phone talking about all the possibilities, he was going in for an appointment tomorrow. Romeo had just started a new rock magazine like Rolling Stone, only a New York version. Scott was sure Romeo would give him a job. It was time to be a real writer and write and write and write and not just sit around in coffeehouses talking about the books he would never write.

Scott got the job writing for the new mag called Climax and his obsession with love interests dwindled the more he hit the keys of his Royal Futura typewriter. But this is a love story and supposed to be about his summer of love. He met girls at the mag, Eileen was provocative, Linda, Southern and charming, Diane very sexy but just not his type. They weren't the one and he knew he had mended his way. He wanted someone or something different. He was tired of bedhopping, the ludicrous term Ralph and Shulie used to describe his love life.

One day, sitting at his makeshift desk (a door on sawhorses) something happened that changed all that. Scott was gazing out the window just staring off into space, and not doing anything in particular. It was a lazy summer day and the heat while suffocating was a bit intoxicating.

He hadn't slept much the night before – Ralph and Shulie had really gotten it on, and their moans were still echoing in his brain. It was a wonder how they lived together like that, Jerry and Scott being single and all. Shulie did not help things. She was born naked and decided she should live her life that way. Shulie's long thick, thick black hair was down to her waist. Her body seemed perfectly formed as if a sculptor had created her as the highest level of female divinity. There was an air about her that her nakedness only enhanced. She seemed to walk on tiptoe not wanting to disturb the ecological balance of the universe. Every man was in love with her, some so jealous of Ralph as they snuck furtive looks. But Ralph was a big guy with a temper to match and the looks looked away rather rapidly.

Scott had memories of Shulie that he would bring out like a set of baseball cards. They all centered on Shulie in the bath. There was the time they talked while she bathed sponging her languid body with soap and he could see to the bottom of the tub and everything in between. There were gorgeous shots of Shulie laying in repose in the big bathtub her hair drifting on the water her breasts just below the surface, enough to titillate the most jaded adventurer. Watching her emerge from the tub, the water cascading off her body, rivulets of moistness silently making their way down her lushness was an experience he would never forget. Her hair formed around her clinging to her nudity, making her even more desirable had she been fully displayed.

These were memory stills and moving pictures a gallery of Shulie embedded in his mind. He constantly had to remind himself that she was Ralph's girl. They were only memories, secret treasures that he would take out on nostalgic occasions

But it was the summer of love and Scott was without love at that moment and after a night of listening to Ralph and Shulie, he knew something was missing, he could still feel the hunger. Scott promised himself that next time it would be different. Not that his mantra helped but it was consoling to a degree. He sat in his loneliness, until he heard a voice shouting in the distance.

"Jerry! Jerry! Jerry!"

Scott went to the window and looked out into a neighborhood that always depressed him but what he now saw lit a spark in his soul. She was blond and he thought to himself blue-eyed. She continued to scream for his friend Jerry. At least he thought it must be for him, he was the only Jerry in the building. Feeling brave Scott raised the window.

"Hey!

She stopped screaming for a minute and looked up at him.

"You're not Jerry," she said.

"No, but he's, my friend."

She was beautiful and he wished he was Jerry.

"I could be Jerry if you wanted me to be Jerry," Scott quickly replied.

"You're not Jerry," she said again.

She was so saucy looking, her innocent face with delightful smile; her stance provocative as she looked up at him. One foot slightly forward, it was a very sexy slouch, to him the ultimate come on. She just seemed to beckon Scott to jump out the window and fly to her.

"Jerry's not here, you can come up and wait for him if you want. I'll come down and let you in."

She climbed the front steps and was leaning against the door jamb as he opened the door and invited her up.

My name's Scott what's yours," he stuck out his hand in greeting.

"Kitty." They shook hands as Scott welcomed her to their shabby chateau.

You have heard about love at first sight, how about love at first shake?

Kitty was tall about 5'10". Scott wanted to kiss her nonstop. He started fantasizing about before he let go of her hand. She said to him:

"Make love to me."

A World without Music is like a Cemetery

interview with Angie Mack, creative musical consultant

You live in Grafton, Wisconsin where our earliest blues recordings were made and preserved. Tell us about that legacy and why you choose to have a relationship with it?

I came upon the blues history by chance when a record collector from Oregon sent everyone in Grafton a mail flyer. The flyer said that he was in the area looking for rare blues 78 records. At the time, I was actually living on the same road that the former record factory and pressing plant were on. However, I had never heard of the recording studio and thought that the flyer was a hoax. Because I was a musician working on my first album at the time, my curiosity peaked.

When I did some initial searching on the Internet around 2003, I couldn't find any information online. My next stop was the Grafton Library which contained the book, Paramount's Rise and Fall: A History of the Wisconsin Chair Company Its Recording Activities by Alex van der Tuuk, 2003. I got in touch with the Dutch author and suggested that we make information about the Paramount record label available on the Internet. From there, we began to collect and archive anything and everything that we could relating to the record label, its

subsidiaries, the musicians, and more. We also began networking with people around the world as well as educating locals. We began a volunteer digitization project through the URL paramountshome.org. Because of our innovative, collaborative and exhaustive efforts, we won the 2006 Wisconsin Historical Society website award. The information from our database can be retrieved by utilizing archive.org

On your recent road trip you made several stops to historical musical sites. What are some of the most intriguing places you visited and what did you learn from them?

One of my favorite recent trips was to Clarksdale, MS. I had never been there before. However, I had been reading about the city and its artists for quite some time. I arrived at night and the place looked like an abandoned ghost town. There was a hauntingly beautiful feeling in the air. No other cars or people were on site. When I reached the porch of the famous Ground Zero Blues Club, I was surprised to find a sculpture honoring a famous musician named James "Super Chikan" Johnson. Ironically, his son Danva Johnson played music on my porch for the international Play

Music on the Porch Day in both 2020 and 2021. I did not know that there was a commemoration for his dad in Clarksdale. To see that surprise correlation between my little Grafton House of Blues and Ground Zero Blues Club was quite fun to discover.

Another key place that I visited was the St. Louis Sound exhibit at the Missouri History Museum. Admission was free when I attended. I originally went to see the exhibit of the eight decade musician and Paramount recording artist Henry "The Mule" Townsend. The exhibit has his original piano, a baby blue performance suit and other artifacts on display. Henry Townsend is the first person inducted into the Paramount Plaza Walk of Fame in Grafton, WI of which I have been the Chairperson since 2006.

Other favorite stops included New Orleans and Austin Texas.

Music is said to soothe the savage breast. These are the words of a poet. Without music life would be a mistake. These are the words of a philosopher. What are the words of a musician, especially yourself, about the humanity within music?

Music allows for human emotion to be heard. Due to a variety of internal as well as external factors throughout my lifetime, I have often felt that my voice didn't matter. There were also times where my emotions were so extreme that I could not find words to express myself. Music has been a healing force in my own life. I have also witnessed music as a healing force in others' lives. I am thankful to be a longtime facilitator of such healing.

How do you reconcile your love for creating with the act of teaching others? Can teaching others infringe on their creative ability?

My teaching style uses a student-led approach and I believe that people learn music in different ways.. I also believe that people are more apt to remember, practice and learn when it involves something that they are interested in. Therefore, I like to take whatever a student might currently know and build off of that.

Some people might thrive as visual learners while others might thrive as auditory learners. My versatility with teaching thousands of students of all ages over the years has allowed me to be uniquely keen as an instructor. I excel in tapping into what little knowledge a student might have and expanding upon that. I highly value innovation and creativity when it comes to learning music. By no means am I a traditional music instructor, therefore, my teaching style never hinders someone's own creative bent.

What have you found most fundamental in pursuit of the arts generally? How can a budding musician prepare themselves?

I would say that the most important pursuit in music is to understand that music is a universal language. Anyone can do something with music. It's just a matter of getting over preconceived notions of what music is. My opinion is that if you can make any sound, it is music. A strong desire to learn and experiment with sound is also beneficial. If someone is looking to bring their musical talent to the next level, a talent coach such as myself can make all of the difference. I can be reached at angie@ozaukeetalent.com if anyone is looking for a little more inspiration. My one-on-one coaching can be done online via Zoom. My personal portfolio can be found at angiemackcreative.com.

The Weeping Boy by Prosper Ifeanyi

Short Fiction

Like a genie, it is one thing to stroke the lamp of love and summon love itself, and it is another to watch that same love go in the manner which it came. Such was the case with our ménage when Papa lost his job: the love left. I still remember that day like it was yesterday. The night was gelid as Chuka and I laid on our mat, I could still hear him sob gently even as he looked the other way to hide his teary eyes. I was still shocked by his actions; we had just finished playing that evening, when I mistakenly gave him a swollen eye in the bathroom. It didn't seem like anything at first, we were only playing and applying water to our juvenile bodies, when he playfully spanked my butt, in my defense, I tried retaliating when I inadvertently shoved his face towards the concrete wall, when he screamed and contorted his face in pain, I thought he was only faking it like we usually did when we overpowered each other. I didn't know how serious this was until we dried our bodies with our shrunken towel, which Mama told me was Chuka's baby shower gift. It was small, stale and I considered myself deshabille when I tied it around my waist. I was about applying the talcum powder to his neck when I noticed his swollen eye, I was scared because of how big and ugly his face had gotten. Alarmed, I boiled water and soaked a piece of Mama's wrapper in it, which I used in massaging his face. I didn't want Mama to see this because she usually was the first to come back home from work. Papa always came home last, and besides, Papa never flogged us, only Mama did. Pressing his face with hot water didn't help matters, although I continued assuring myself that it was lessening, I too had begun to cry.

The first lesson I learnt that day was: miracles did exist. Miracles existed, and I witnessed them first-hand. The first was, Papa came back from work earlier than Mama that day. This was very surprising and perplexing, I froze where I stood, and at that moment, I don't know why, but I remembered replaying the song "body go tell you o" by Burnaboy inside my head. But there was something about Papa that day, something gloomy, something forlorn, something sad about his eyes. He confirmed my assumption by calling my full name that day.

"Chibuzor!" See that was the problem, he never called me Chibuzor, he only called me Uzo or Buzo. By now he had seen Chuka's swollen eye and was very angry about it, he called us out to the parlour and instructed us to lie on the floor. We were always scared of lying on the floor, Chuka and me, we preferred you just flogged us there and now for we hated suspense. Then Papa came with his belt from the room and uttered five words which I don't think I will forget in a hurry.

"Who did this to you?"

Those were the words. I wanted to shit or take a leak on my patched short. I was in great trepidation because my Papa hadn't flogged any of us before—I felt like I would die if he did. With Chuka gazing at me through his shiner, and back at my father, I knew I didn't stand a chance, but then, I witnessed my second miracle.

"I...I slid on my way to fetch water, Papa," he muttered slowly. Those words coming from Chuka plunged through my heart; it felt like the biggest favour anyone had done for me, I felt like hugging him dearly, but my freedom was pyrrhic, for it came at a great cost. I was dismissed into the room, but from where I hid, I could see Papa flog his bare arse and him shouting on top of his voice. "How many is it?" Asked Papa furiously.

"Twelve...no fourteen," he screamed and writhed with crazed frenzy.

I was crying too now, I felt like I had betrayed my brother and I knew I would never stand up for him like that—not when something as important as my butt was at stake. It took lots of courage, something I didn't have. After caning him, my brother joined me in the room, all I could do was embrace him and whisper sweet words into his ears, I expressed how sorry I was, even when I knew it wasn't enough. There was something off about my father, I could hear him complain bitterly about the government, he blamed Chuka's accident on the oil which was being drilled by the government in the stream where we fetched water. You see the government brought these whitemen to explore oil in our streams, they claimed our streams were rich in natural gases, but succeeded in polluting our waters and contaminating our fishes, and the government did nothing about it. A boy named Odume had broken his neck on one of those occasions, when he tried carrying his pail of water through the oily paths. The engineers at the site claimed that Odume walked through the steepy paths of the stream, but we knew they were lying, and that the oil was responsible for his fate. I still didn't understand my Papa's angle from the whole thing, my Papa wasn't a sourpuss, so I wondered where all of this was coming from. It all became clearer that night, when Mama came back from work. They spoke in low tones, but I couldn't fail to overhear Papa mention that he had lost his security job in a site where an oil well was sunk.

It was a gelid night, so much filled my mind, I wondered which was worse: Chuka receiving my comeuppance, or Papa losing his job.

***

How a group of workers lost their jobs en masse in an oil well site still wasn't what baffled me, what ate me deep was the fact that home was altogether in shambles. Since Papa lost his job Mama no longer paid attention to him. Sometimes, she would eat at work and get moi-moi for me and Chuka at night. One those occasions, we dared not ask what Papa would eat. Mama's trouble was far worse than that of Papa, it was deafening, excruciating, longer—she would nag and stress the issue till you waned. That was the same way she nagged Papa about getting a job.

Sometimes, she tried to be understanding, she would quarrel Papa into going out to look for a job, but most of the times he came back looking dejected; it was either each

company or factory didn't need his security expertise, or they felt he was too old. Even rejection too can do the most to a human, so Papa stopped going to search for jobs. Twice, Mama had given him money for transport to scout for jobs; the first time, he used the money in buying a new radio which he hung beside a wall clock which had stopped working for over a year. He would put on the radio each time Mama left the house for work because he didn't want her to find out, we didn't tell Mama because we loved the sound the little box emitted, and that was I and Chuka's little secret. We loved listening to matches from the radio and I always loved it when Liverpool were the ones playing, I was a Liverpool fan. Mama later found out about the radio, I don't know how up till today, but what I do know is that it didn't end well for Papa or the radio. She smashed the radio into pieces and the peripheries flew East and West and some even rolled under our chair; that day, Chuka and I had scavenged innards of what was left of the radio to see if we could get magnets and tapes for our kite. She rained abuses on Papa for that week and I didn't even know how they made up because Papa began eating eba with us again in the same bowl. That brings me to the second time she gave him money for his job hunt, this time, Papa would wait for Mama to go to work then sneak back in to sleep, he ended up using the money to play Bet9ja and he always lost, horribly. I know he didn't go to search for work because on several occasions I came back home from school because I always forgot my mathematics textbook— I always forgot maths and not english, I didn't like maths very much—and on those occasions, I'd catch him sleeping. I also know he always lost his bets because I and Chuka sometimes

help him in predicating matches and staking games. He would ask:

"Who will win between Liverpool and Chelsea?"

And I would always pick Liverpool, because I loved Mohammed Salah— maybe because he was a left footed player, and so was I. Mama didn't really get what Papa was doing until she caught him herself in one of those Betting houses, that day was a very significant day because since Papa started playing bet, he had never won, but that day was different, he had finally won a whopping sum of one million naira, enough money to change our lives; that was when Mama went into the gaming house to tear his evidence slip, she tore his clothes and mortified him among his peers who surrounded him to congratulate his feat. That was the day Mama was labeled "the evil lady" people insulted her and called her an ingrate, they called her hot-tempered, badly behaved and even a virago—I didn't know what a virago was but I guessed it was a hurtful thing to say to a woman. That was also the first time I cried without being flogged or hurt by someone, I cried because although my juvenile mind couldn't comprehend or picture what one million naira looked like, I knew it was a lot of money that just went through the drain.

How, you might ask, did Papa get through this? Well, he never did. In fact, that was when he started complaining about being hypertensive; he would sleep and shiver all day in bed. He didn't speak to anyone, or eat anything, he would get up and walk around the compound a little then go back to sleep. For a man that just lost one million naira, he sure looked very scrawny and old. He became hostile and unfriendly, he didn't talk to Mama or help Chuka to do his assignments anymore, I was young, but I sure knew hate in the eyes of an adult when I saw one. He still played bets sometimes, but he didn't win a thing, sometimes he didn't even like to show his face in the gaming house because of the whole fiasco Mama had pulled on that day. It was even disturbing to know that Papa didn't even come home at night anymore, he would catch up with some group of friends and they would drink till dawn. They talked about politics, their predicaments and their wives. I even had the impression that Papa no longer wanted Mama for a wife again, it was disheartening.

Mama on the other hand was having her fair share of the troubles, she was either called at the market or at home to come pick Papa from a bar, or at a gutter. The women who bought the wares she sold no longer came like before, some even gossiped her and called her an enemy of progress, things were funny like that. As hard as it was, I still wondered how I managed to do well in school. With all of that going on, even the most sanest man alive would lose his sanity. I am muddled, I am disarrayed—I mean, what child wouldn't? It's not everyday a child grows up around an overbearing matriarch, neither is it everyday one's father loses his job and certainly not everyday one's brother becomes his keeper. So many people, so many faces, so many problems; this is my reality and if you have a better story, I would like to hear it.

Texture of a Sari

Toufiq Zohur

Eyes were fixed on the Tajmahal road

through the veil of noon.

A humble love there in the folds of a sari

I looked from a distance and don't hold her hands.

I decided to give her a rose

And the sari turned into a green tree

The leaves as if were the Mola fish of ancient charyapada

The mighty waves of sea fell on the upper part of the sari

And I was thrilled by the five feet and two inches fire.

I looked upon the sari with the thirst of a sea

And drowned under the shadow of her eyes.

I saw this tree in Sobhanbagh first in the wet sun

Then I saw her fresh in the morning sky

Gradually I saw her peacock shape in turquoise colour.

By pressing the carousel of trust,

I suddenly discovered the fragrance

of mystery with the touch of my lips.

Since then, with the earthy smell I realized

The pigeons in my breath keep flying

In a rain-soaked field

You are my mirror

Where you stand in the texture of a sari.

Jaydeep Sarangi
From Dulung to Beas: Flow of the Soul
Poetry
Authorspress, 2021
ISBN (Paperback) 978-81-7273-646-0
Pp 83 | Price 295

These fifty-one poems deal with varied themes – history, society, existential angst, and global fraternity. The predominating image is that of the river whose generosity remains intact despite human ingratitude. Postcolonial and eco-spiritual, the collection advocates an engaged detachment with life. Available via Amazon.

Good Enough for Me

Melissa Chappell writes on the difficulty of writing with limited income

Writing. It's what I live for. It's what I crave. I hunger for it. I strive to improve upon it. It is my air and nourishment. The ground beneath my feet. It is second only to God. And yet I can't really *live it* in the way that I want to live it. It is impossible for many poets because poetry is impossibly un-marketable. No one is reading it. No one sees what we poets see in it: the aesthetic qualities, the language that startles, mystifies and explodes on the page. The subtle rhythms that invite one into the poem– suddenly the reader is one with the flow, like floating on the unbreaking waves of the ocean. Sometimes it is riotous like a river, taking the reader to parts unknown. Poetry is beyond what words can describe. As Auden said, "Poetry doesn't cause events to happen. Poetry is an event in itself." This is what I love being a part of, and what I will be a part of for as long as I have breath. Other writers know as well as I do that it's not just a hobby. It's life.

Yet I want it to be more. I would love to make a living at it. To teach. To share this passion with others in an organized way, and get paid for it! To do workshops, perhaps. I would love to go back to school and get a Masters in English or an MFA, but for personal reasons I would not be able to pay back the debt. Even if you were able to go back to school and teach, the pay is so paltry you'd still be shopping for discounts at Food Lion. But that doesn't matter. I would do it anyway, because I'd be doing what I loved. I would just like to be published more. Yet there are so many barriers. Many of the publishing houses are only accepting through contests. And I have about as much chance of being published through a contest as Vladimir Putin has of smiling. Also, the fees that these contests charge are ungodly. Twenty and thirty dollars to enter something I don't really have a shot at winning is just a waste of my money, especially since I'm on disability. There are fees for everything. When I have four dollars in the bank, I can't afford to send in a submission for three dollars unless I'm one of the Flying Wallendas and willing to take a fall in my account. What is a reading fee, anyway? I think that publishers put "reading fees" there so they won't be inundated with the poetry of just anyone and everyone. It is their choice, but it excludes those who are financially volatile, and who may have a lot to say.

In addition, so many things are *themed*. I don't do well with writing to a theme, or a prompt, or a picture or anything like that. Call it having no imagination, if you will, but it's just not my mode of being as far as a writer is concerned. Just give me my books to read, a computer and Google Docs and leave me to write. A theme will come from my muse, which is music. (These days, Stephanie Jones' classical guitar rendition of "Blowin in the Wind").

Writing helps me forget about the money, which I don't have. It helps me to forget about a lot of things, which I don't have. But it helps me remember a lot of things that I do have: Close poet friends and a place in the growing poetry community. And the freedom to write. That's good enough for me.

Melissa A. Chappell is a native of South Carolina. She has a BA in music theory and an MDiv. Besides being a writer, she plays the piano and performs on the guitar, lute, and as a vocalist. She shares her life with her family and two miniature schnauzers.

I Can't Live Without *POP*, Anymore!

World Inkers interviews *Annette Tarpley*, founder of *The Passion of Poetry*

Why did you start The Passion of Poetry?

I was on a poetry site one day and a negative comment was left. On a whim...I decided to create my own site where a positive environment would reign. One in which acceptance and encouragement would be the foundation in which writers/and poets could grow, hone their skills, and become better poets in a positive platform. I am a strong proponent in the belief that negativity breeds negativity, and positivity gives birth to positivity.

Why is it called The Passion of Poetry instead of The Passion in Poetry? Or another name?

It is the name that immediately popped into my head. The passion of poetry is evidenced by the ink that bleeds from the poet's pen. Poetry lends to an avenue and means by which we can freely express. I believe it has no constraints, that the mind can creatively conjure a plethora of ways for the poet to express his word art. The passion of poetry is an entity, which is felt in the for passion we have FOR it, and that is displayed IN the contents therein.

What did you want to say with the name of the group?

That it is our passion for poetry serves as the underlying catalyst for creatively expressing. It is our passion that steers us to continually write...many of us doing so in a prolific manner. Without passion in our creative expression, we are left to works that appeal to an audience of one...ourselves. It is important that there is clarity in our writing. In other words, do not speak in riddles so complex that your reader is not able to interpret the content of your work.

Public group postings of poetry are considered published by the poetry journals. Is that ever an obstacle to your group dynamics and advancement?

It is my personal view that there exists some ambiguity on whether posting a poem to a Facebook site, is truly considered publishing. There appears to be a mixture of opinion. One publisher may tell me yes, the other no. There does not appear to be one major consensus across the board. In cases such as this, I submit according to their requirements of whether they are accepting published or unpublished works, and honor that publisher's interpretation and submission criteria.

What role do the arts play in your life, other than writing and sharing poetry online? Do you have other passions in the arts?

I have always loved and appreciated the arts. I consider myself overall, l to be rather creative and artistic in nature. I love art and have a true appreciation for it. Often someone's art inspires me to write. The picture or painting speaks to me, and I can create poetry as a result of their marvelous works. I have always loved the theater. I love to go to plays/productions, both locally and when I travel to a city that has theatrical events. I have a love for music, almost every genre. Songs are really poetry accompanied by music. I aspire to someday write the lyrics for a song. I actually have written one. I also love dance and have attended ballets in the past. So, to sum it up, I have a great love for the arts and embrace the passion and creative expression of others who possess those talents.

What do you consider the root of passion? How is it related to creating beautiful works of literature in your opinion?

I have always been acutely aware that a writer resides within me. After graduating from high school, I either wanted to be a writer/journalist, or a nurse. For the past 40 years I have been involved in my nursing career. Often working full time and simultaneously going back to school to further my education. I have master's degree in science and currently work as a nurse practitioner. Yet, not fulfilling the desires that I had for writing has always haunted me. Two years ago, I really found my love and passion for it, and have been writing ever since. In December of 2021, I wrote my first short story, which was published in a book two weeks later. Since then, I have written two more short stories, both of which have been accepted for publication. The root of my passion for writing and literature has always been present, just hibernating all these years waiting to be unleashed. It has always been my desire to write a novel. I have started the first two chapters of one, based upon my Poem, "The Ballad of Ned," which is about bullying. I also have written a couple of poems that I would like to turn into children's books. The ability for us to produce great works of literature, resides in our burning passion within. Passion is the underlying current that gives us the creative ability to produce beautiful works of literature.

What was your proudest moment in publication?

I think that my proudest moment in publication thus far, will be when my short story about my grandmother is published, within the next month. But my ultimate proudest moment lies waiting behind the curtain's backstage. It will be the first novel that I produce, a long-awaited dream, coming into fruition.

What do you anticipate from The Passion of Poetry in the near future?

I anticipate that we will continue to grow and thrive as a welcoming forum, where poets can continue to hone their skills and write stellar pieces. At over 19,000 members in less than two years, its growth continues to amaze me. I believe we offer more writing contests and opportunities than any other poetry community that I have encountered. I have recently built a stand-alone website, POPSTAR Poetry, in which we are and will continue to publish the beautiful works of our members. POP has a close-knit feel, we are a family, and I want the poets to call it their home, but beyond that…FEEL it is their home!

BOOK REVIEW

Lustus: The Prince of Darkness
by Dr. Jernail Sing Anand
Review by Dr. Maqsood Jafri

Lustus: The Prince of Darkness is an epic poem written by Dr. Jernail Sing Anand. His six epics have been already published and it is his seventh book. He is internationally known and leading world poet and philosopher whom Global Literary Icon Dr. Maja Herman Sekulic has described as "One of the greatest philosophers among poets, and one of the greatest poets among philosophers." He has sought my opinion on his epic. I found this epic so interesting that I read it word to word and was highly impressed and amazed on his imaginative and creative power. The source of poetry is passion and the fountain of philosophy is reason. When passion and reason blend, they emanate a poet- philosopher and are incarnated in the form of Dr. Anand. Besides, being a great erudite and savant, he is the chairman of many international literary and academic fora and a recipient of several awards. He is a reformer and revolutionary. The diction of his epic is simple, facile and charming. The poem is insightful, inspiring, gravitating, captivating and capturing. It encompasses the social, political, religious and moral decadence of our modern age. English poetry has many genres and forms such as panegyric, pastoral poetry, ballad, sonnet, ode, lyric, elegy, blank verse and free verse. What is an epic poem? Aristotle in his book entitled *The Poetics* in part 5 defines epic as one of the forms of poetry, contrasted with lyric poetry and with drama in the form of tragedy or comedy. The famous examples of epic poetry include the Sumerian *Epic of Gilgamesh*, the ancient Indian *Mahabharata, Ramayana* in Sanskrit, *Shahnama of Firdusi* in Persian, the Ancient Greek *Odyssey* and *Iliad*, of Homer, Virgil's *Aeneid*, Dante's *Divine Comedy*, John Milton's *Paradise Lost*, Alexander Pope's "The Rape of the Lock", and the modern epic *The Cantos* by Ezra Pound.

The epic titled *Lustus : The Prince of Darkness* written by Dr. Anand is a neo- mythological epic. It is a sequel to *Paradise Lost* of John Milton. Satan beguiles Eve and dwindles her faith and both Adam and Eve touch the prohibited tree and eat its fruit and are damned.

In a play titled *Dr. Faustus* written by Marlowe, we also find Beelzebub mastering over the soul of Dr. Faustus and tempting him for pelf and power. Dr. Faustus had sold his soul to Satan and his sacrilegious ideas eventually make him the replica and embodiment of divine condemnation and curse. He faces a miserable death cursed and condemned by divine agents. In the epic of Dr. Anand, we find the majority of the modern humans have sold their souls to Satan for worldly material gains. Satan has grown old, so he anoints his cousin Lustus and transfers his obnoxious and vile mission to this big "Corporate Evil." Like the Satan in the epic of Milton, we find Satan and his successor Lustus challenging the authority and sovereignty of God. The following are the main characters in this epic: Greda is the goddess of greed. Amazinia is the daughter of Satan. Other characters are Kal, Narad, Kuru, Brahma, Vishnu, Indra, Sita, Beelzebub, Santez, Denzy, Singer, and Faustus. All play a specific role assigned to them.

Lustus is enmeshed in psychic pride of having " Excessive Knowledge". The author opines as the excessive light blinds us, Lustus gets astray from the right path and his arrogance does not emit light but casts darkness. He is entrapped and wrapped up in the cloak of the lengthening shadows of infidelity and arrogance. The story of this epic picks up "Ravana", who had ten heads, meaning excess of knowledge and maneuvered to abduct "Sita", and courts his own destruction. Lustus on his becoming the Prince of Darkness addresses the world and gives his own contrived devilish and sacrilegious "Ten Commandments ", quite contrary to the holy " Ten Commandments" given by prophet Moses in The Torah. He announces his pugnacious Satanic Mission against the Divine Mission. This epic is not a humorous , amorous and sunny poem like the epic of Alexander Pope, in which sylphs and nymphs appear to safe and succor Belinda whose lock was cut. Dr. Anand has a reformatory mission like John Milton. Milton aspired to show the ways of God to Man. Dr. Anand criticizes the modern man, who has ample electronic and scientific knowledge but no spark of nobility, divinity , sanity, sacrifice, and humanity. This modern education has made man like a robot who has no compassion and love for others and is confined in the cell of his ego as an arrogant and tyrant species. Lustus is an embodiment of lust for power, wealth and sexual extravagance. These vices are the quest of our modern man. The author is much concerned about the vicious modes and mores of modern society. There is a war between the demons and gods. As in the *Paradise Regained* of Milton, we find Jesus Christ as a savior and redeemer, in this epic we find the victory of God over Satan with the spiritual succor of "Durga." In content and spirit this Epic differs from some ancient mythological epics as it commensurates a new spirit of real human political and social issues and unveils spiritual decadence of the so called custodians of faiths in the form of saints and priests. It also unmasks the gruesome faces of politicians, businessmen, educators, government officials and journalists.

Lustus plans to create disorder in the cosmic plan as well. By the help of modern science, he intends to change the natural properties and traits of birds, trees, and animals and free them from their corporal nature and provide them copious freedom from the yoke of godly controlled arena. His weird plan is to impart super consciousness to animals, birds, and plants as well as to those who behave below dignity like humans. Such genius is called evil genius. Actually, the modern knowledge without vision, empathy, compassion and concern for human noble values is the ingenuity and contrivance of devilish mindset. People have become selfish, cruel and callous. A war with God ensues in which Lustus challenges God and shows his great array of armies of "Night", the teachers, politicians religionists, students and technocrats and asks God who are with him? This mischievous challenge unnerves "gods" and they send "Durga", a goddess to kill them. She kills several of the monsters. Eventually, there is a truce between both armies for cease- fire after several setbacks and bloodshed.

This epic consists of 12 cantos. In each canto, the author gives a specific message. It is a neo-mythology and represents our age in all its weirdness. The core message of this epic is that modern Scientific knowledge is being misused and that has created immense disaster and destruction to mankind. The tag line of the epic is:

"The more we know,
the more miserable we grow."

Does it mean the author is retrogressive and is afraid of enlightenment and scientific knowledge? Not at all. How can a man of vision, sagacity and sanity be retrogressive in his poetic mission? Like Dr. Iqbal, he condemns the modern science, self adoration, self- conceited psychic shows and modern shameless culture that lead humans to exploitative mindset and are void of human passion. The eyes are dazzled by the excess of this blurring light. We see a singer who appears and in his song unveils numerous social evils. He sings:

"O; temples, shrines, mosques,
Where they discuss politics.
Oh; God.
Do they too believe in Devil."

On page 26 of the epic the Author highlights the vicious mission of Lustus and that is to disrupt and destroy the authority of God and establish the Sovereignty of Satan. The prophets claimed to establish the Kingdom of God on earth, while Lustus announces the establishment of the Kingdom of Darkness. The odious odium of Satan against the divine mission of God surpasses all boundaries and yearns to distract and dissipate men by Satanic dissimulation which is nothing but to dissociate and discord humans. In Canto 4, we see at the "Park of Passion", Lustus bows before Greda, the goddess of Greed. Satan tells Lustus to seek the blessings of Greda. At the shrine of Greda, voices announce:

"Hail lust, hail Deceit, hail Duplicity, hail Desire, hail Revenge, hail Fire".

So this is the mission of Satan and Lustus. In this Canto, Dr. Anand criticizes the Western Imperialists who have robbed humans and ruled mercilessly over weaker nations. While addressing the world leaders, Faustus who is the neo- corporate is not only targeting the visible world , the real assault is on virtual mind , the air, the soul, and the consciousness of mankind. He announces to corporatize and finally imperialize. The author criticizes the Western Culture as well which has made modern women rebellious to the extent that they neither need a husband, nor home life, and in the name of so-called liberty and modern education and feminism have crossed the boundaries of civility and morality. This modern culture has vanquished the family system, and love and respect for elders. In Europe, the woman dominates the man and this unnatural and unbalanced way of life has created immense problems. The divorces are in vogue. A generation of profligate, half castes and bastards is in rampancy. This is the World of Darkness. In Canto 5, we see Lustus preaching terrorism, bloodbath, lesbianism, and to vanquish human individuality and self respect. In Canto 6, he criticizes the beauty contests and hate culture promoted by Lustus who proclaims to uproot the culture of compassion, peace and forgiveness and instructs the women in these lines:

"Don't bother about husbands,
Make them look after the kids and your kitchen".

In this Canto, Lustus directs Amazinia to work to end goodness, honesty, genuineness, character, authenticity, transparency, religiosity, godliness and chastity.

In Cantos 7 to Canto 12, we find Lustus prompting and promoting his vile, vindictive and virulent agenda. His mission is to promote the holy places in which the demon incarnate priests and saints should promote extremism, religious and racial discrimination and sectarianism. To darken the Empire of Light, Satan needs his agents in temples, synagogues, mosques and churches. Sex perversion, yellow journalism, and free sex culture must be promoted. Lustus addresses the "Parliament of Devils" and tells them that God is planning to send Lord Krishna or some powerful Man to save the earth. But we are well prepared to face his any apostle. Brahma discusses the battle and redemption issue with Indra and Vishnu. They see the earth with a telescope to examine the situation. They see that the earth is full of sin and see ravages and gang-rapes by the upper class and no one is punished. A girl named "Heer" is not permitted to marry her suitor "Ranjha" and forced marriages are imposed on innocent loving young couples.

While concluding the Epic, we see that the army of demons is defeated by the army of angels and through a Truce, the battle is ended with some conditions agreed by the both parties. Lustus, cunningly agrees not to interfere in the divine mission of God, but secretly plans to continue his mission.

The gods and goddesses confess that the demons have provided all resources of merriment to the people in a negative way and we have not cared for their genuine rights and demands and this is the reason that majority of the people have been derailed. Hence, the gods decide to take practical steps to ease and appease humans as dry sermons are not sufficient. The thirst can only be quenched by water; not by a mirage or promises. Lustus accepts his defeat but with a new vigorous zeal and zest claims that he will continue to distract humans from divine path as the majority of humans find pleasure in sin and only a few stick to virtue. Vice is sweet and virtue sour. But he has forgotten the Words of the Bible that noble people are the Salt of the earth. Lustus is questioned by one of his disciples that in the presence of Gita, The Torah, The Bible and The Quran, how his manifesto will be enshrined and accepted by people? He retorts that the followers of these holy books have distorted the real message of these books and do not act upon the spirit of religion, so we need not worry. They only pay lip service to religion and their spiritual and religious mentors and guides are imposters and become professional. Hence, we will definitely succeed in our mission.

The Moral of the epic is the victory of virtue over vice. In the "Cosmic Voice", which is found in the Cantos, there is a message of harmony, peace, and human equality through the cosmic scheme. The safety of birds and beasts is also desired with the safety of humankind. The moral of the epic is summed up by the author himself. He writes:

"It is a work of fiction, and I have tried to create a new myth which is commensurate with the modern times. Lustus is a neo- mythical being, who is most natural evolution in the evil ranks. The fight is metaphorical and it is my faith that Lustus cannot be finished, only he can be silenced, because good and evil co- exist and man must learn how to maintain a balance of the twin impulses which determine human conduct for better or worse"

Aristotle in his book titled *The Poetics* says that every play and literary work must end showing the victory of virtue and defeat of vice so that human society is purged from ills and evils. Great literary scholars and poets like Dr. Johnson, T. S. Eliot, Sheikh Sadi, Dr. Iqbal and Altaf Hussain Hali promoted didacticism in literature to change the world by making it the

Kingdom of God which is the Kingdom of Light. The Kingdom of Satan is the Kingdom of Darkness. I feel it pertinent to proclaim that like John Milton whose *Paradise Regained* shows us the Ways of God to Man; similarly, *Lustus: The Prince of Darkness* of Dr. Jernail Sing Anand takes us out from the dark and dreary dungeons of evil and shows us the bright Ways of God to Man.

New York

February 1, 2022

Dr. Maqsood Jafri, Ph.D in English literature and D.Phil in Philosophy, author of 30 books of poetry and prose, is a poet, scholar, orator, columnist, educator and political and civil rights activist based in New York. He has written poetry in seven languages Viz; English, Arabic, Persian, Urdu, Kashmiri, Punjabi and Poonchi.

How I Spread the Inks of Kindness, Even in Pain
Interview with *Jill Sharon Kimmelman*

Even before coronavirus unsettled the world, creative people have confronted struggles beyond their control. What are your own struggles and how have you managed them to release your first collection of poetry?

My own struggles, throughout my entire adult life, have been related to my physical health.

When I was 24, I contracted a virus, guillane barre syndrome.

It paralyzed all the muscles in my body & landed me on a ventilator. I was awake & aware of everything, however, due to the breathing tube, I was unable to respond. Being conscious on a ventilator is my definition of hell on earth.

My recovery was termed excellent, leaving me with little residual weakness. Twenty years later, I suffered a relapse of guillane barre syndrome. This time, I was left with lifetime symptoms, including an increase of severe fibromyalgia issues, along with multiple additional health conditions.

Less than 1 year after recovering from guillane barre syndrome, I endured 6 endometriosis-related surgeries in a period of 13 months. There was nothing that could control the endometriosis from strangling my organs, so the sad decision was made to have a complete hysterectomy at the age of 27.

Waking up in the recovery room, I experienced my very first chronic intractable migraine, a condition that is hereditary, debilitating & with me every day of my life.

This part of my story has a joyous ending.

A year later, almost to the day, I was standing in a labor & delivery room, holding the hand of a young woman, age 17, who had chosen us to be the parents of the baby boy she was moments away from bringing into the world. Her mom was holding her other hand. The nurse handed our son Jordan to me & was asked by the dr to cut the umbilical cord. Moments like these are as rare as they are precious.

God, or whatever higher power we find ourselves pleading with & shaking our helpless fists, may pile on the obstacles, stacking them so high & dense, that we feel lost & overwhelmed. Holding my new son in my arms for the very first time helped put it all in perspective.

I have learned to accept the challenge of living with severe health limitations, recognizing the role they play in every moment, how much or how little control I have over them, & the blessing of so very many lessons learned from these conditions, those I no longer curse & rail against.

In the years that followed my son's birth & the burgeoning popularity of my own business in the culinary arts arena, my physical health deteriorated, I was diagnosed with two auto immune diseases, & was forced to retire in the early years of this century. What felt like a dead end were actually pangs of longing & excitement—a desire to connect with the writer in me, more specifically, the poet who last played any part in my life since college.

How can creative minds work around their own difficulties? Do you ever feel that your struggles with health impede your progress as a poet?

The key to that question is understanding that the creative mind, when feeling overwhelmed & frustrated, is still CREATIVE & will approach each incident, interruption & inconvenience related to the creative process with CREATIVITY rather than logic.

My struggles with physical health could indeed impede my progress as a poet if I allowed it. I do not. I never will.

I use my own history, current situation, & a sincere desire to promote optimistic thinking, in a time of ever-encroaching darkness & extreme polarization, to instill in my reader's, a belief in everyday miracles, precious moments of celebration & sadness, the beauty & bounty of all we share in our daily lives.

As poets we are charged to use our poet's voices to initiate change, to shine light on issues of critical significance, offer insight & illumination in times where isolation is very common & no one is unscathed from this global pandemic, the world calls Corona, changing our lives, world-wide forever.

Every task takes longer when your day begins with severe pain & the struggle to be productive. It is often the simplest of activities that leads to a teeth-gnashing siege of unbearable pain. Taking a shower, but one item on a "to do list", can be so draining that I am forced to shift my entire scheduled day, postpone the goals that seemed so easy as I filled them into my week's calendar.

Writing my first book, *You Are The Poem*, released in early November 2021, was one of the greatest challenges of my life.

I was hospitalized 4 times in the 8 months that it took to compile the poems, edit-revise-edit, deter-mine each poem's position within 3-themed collections, create bold full color collages as entryways to each collection, & work closely with my husband Tim Little, hospitalized since late April of 2021, He remained an inpatient for close to 8 months together, before visiting restrictions were changed, we worked together to outline target marketing ideas. They included online & local opportunities. Every single concept has been a success!

While putting together the manuscript for my first book, I found my lifelong commitment, to maintaining strong organizational skills, was an excellent tool.

I have met & overcome 40 years of battling & learning to live & thrive with chronic health issues. The frequency & intensity of these challenges has served to add dimension & scope to my primarily free-verse poems. It enriches my work to have the elements of empathy & compassion so linked to my words.

Does the feeling that one is not in control of their problems present a different kind of conundrum than problems with easier solutions? How can such difficulties be incorporated into the creative process from your experiences?

Yes there are times when feelings of frustration can be overwhelming. It happens to everyone. As a poet, I use those times to re-focus my energy, still writing but engaged in pursuing a different part of the creative process.

When writing something new isn't pleasing & editing/revising isn't making the impact that I am striving towards, I change my perspective. Instead of pursuing the frustration of a new poem, I may choose to take that time to approach a list of submission resources & spend a few hours preparing 3-4 complete submissions. Some poems are sent to editors who have never turned me down. Others are sent to names of literary journals that I have culled & decided might be a good fit for my work.

It may not be how I planned to spend my day. It may be that the next day, I don't even have as much physical strength as I did the day before, but at least the entire day was not a waste!

It is known you appreciate mentoring and working with young writers. Can you tell us when that started and why? How does it fulfill you as a creative mind?

Yes, I believe that mentoring a young writer is a way that we can give thanks & show our appreciation to those poets who gave their time to us.

There have been marvelous generous poets who have volunteered to review my earlier poetic efforts, shared their wisdom, promoted me on social media & helped me navigate the world of publishing poems versus simply writing, working to perfect my own poetry.

I enjoy a very special relationship with my beloved protege, a 14 year old teen author & poet, Elizabeth O Ogunmodede. The story of how we met is a wonderful example of how amazing it is to be a member of the great big, beautiful, online poetry community, often more like family.

Elizabeth contacted me to request that we meet. Her request concerned the possibility of us working together in an informal student/teacher relationship. After our first zoom meeting with Lizzy, her two younger sisters & her extremely talented dad, I agreed to her suggestion. Almost 18 months later, Lizzy & I are definitely closer than ever.

Mentoring Elizabeth has been pure JOY. Our roles change from day to day, visit by visit.

Sometimes she is the one educating me about tik tok & building my social media presence. Other times, I am the one answering questions & offering guidance. We learn so much about one another in our visits.

If it wasn't for Lizzy, I would not have an Amazon or Goodreads page/profile.

Without her social media savvy, I would be lost in a tech maze. Without her infectious laughter,

friendship, concern for Tim and me, & the sincere love that our families share, starting with the 2 of us, our lives would never be the same.

Like any activity where we are volunteering to help others, we come to experience a rare pleasure. It is a simple analogy, but barely touches on the true gift at the heart of mentoring.

What qualities differentiate a creative person from someone else? Do other people who struggle seem less optimistic without the creative impulse?

In my humble opinion, I would say that a creative person is successful, in a large part, thanks to a conscious decision to allow daily struggles, with chronic illness, & often unbearable pain, to offer a unique, candid perspective into their poetry.

There are no easy quick-fix solutions or fit-all panaceas when the first thing that I feel every day, what usually awakens me with a dogged determination, is screaming muscle, joint, facial/ cranial, & most days head & belly pain.

Ignoring these things takes just as much, sometimes even more, effort than allowing the intensity of the pain to offer depth, insight & greater originality to my work.

I cannot answer for anyone else who seems to struggle with any less than fully embracing messages crafted into inspired remarkable & memorable poems.

An optimistic demeanor is essential. Physical challenges, especially when aggravated by pain, are daunting. With the unflagging emotional support of a loving partner who has enough belief in my God-given gifts for two people, I am already greatly blessed.

Of course magnificent poems are crafted every day by poets who are not so fortunate. To have a glorious muse, one who inspires our words, elevates our language & enriches our poems, is to be truly blessed.

It is not enough to simply be a poet of merit. It is necessary to continually expose yourself to the work of our contemporary fellow poets as well as the classics. This should include poets whose diverse backgrounds, family, cultural, educational levels, ethnicity & religious beliefs, are of vital importance & aid in increasing the emotion, strength & overall message of our poetry.

This talking point also refers to the regular interaction between myself & "my precious girl", my teen protege Elizabeth O Ogunmodede. Our differences outnumber our similarities by a sizable percentage. Yet it is those all-important shared goals revolving around our mission of a successful poem or book, that matters the most.

How do you encourage creative minds to continue to create during the current hardships we are facing collectively? Is there a way we can still balance individual merit in creativity with seeking common solutions to difficult problems?

When I think about this last set of questions, my mind is drawn to the great many lessons that can be gleaned from other poet's work. How they tackle the tough stuff & challenges is often found in their poetry.

In a luminous intelligently crafted poem written by a creative, confident, & exceptional poet, is where I find the words that sing to me.

Do not let your words go unsaid. Listen to the stories all around you. Be a receiver of life. Tell stories that will resonate within the hearts, minds, & souls of your readers as well as other poets.

I am a huge believer in remaining open-minded. Constructive feedback can be invaluable, if we are willing to accept how simple, but essential modifications, can do a great deal to improve any poem.